P9-CMD-968

UP AND RUNNING

─── W I T H ───

Microsoft Works 3.0

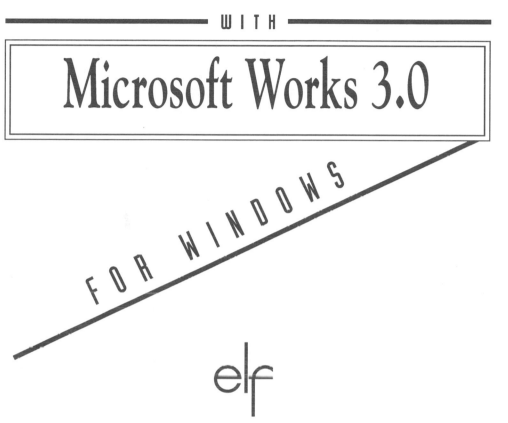

F O R   W I N D O W S

e|f

electronic learning facilitators, inc.

The Dryden Press

Harcourt Brace College Publishers

Fort Worth   Philadelphia   San Diego   New York   Orlando   Austin   San Antonio
Toronto   Montreal   London   Sydney   Tokyo

Publisher	Liz Widdicombe
Executive Editor	Richard Bonacci
Developmental Editor	Traci Keller
Project Editor	Kathryn Stewart
Production Manager	Robert Wright
Book Designer	Bill Brammer
Cover Image	Lamberto Alvarez

Copyright © 1995 by Harcourt Brace & Company

All rights reserved. No part of this publication may be reproduced or transmitted in any form or by any means, electronic or mechanical, including photocopy, recording, or any information storage and retrieval system, without permission in writing from the publisher.

Requests for permission to make copies of any part of the work should be mailed to: Permissions Department, Harcourt Brace & Company, 6277 Sea Harbor Drive, Orlando, FL 32887-6777.

Address for Editorial Correspondence
The Dryden Press, 301 Commerce Street, Suite 3700, Fort Worth, TX 76102

Address for Orders
The Dryden Press, 6277 Sea Harbor Drive, Orlando, FL 32887
1-800-782-4479, or 1-800-433-0001 (in Florida)

ISBN: 0-03-013907-4

Library of Congress Catalogue Number: 94-77833

Printed in the United States of America

5 6 7 8 9 0 1 2 3 4   0 1 8   9 8 7 6 5 4 3 2 1

The Dryden Press
Harcourt Brace College Publishers

Preface

Overview

Up and Running with Works 3.0 for Windows is a comprehensive workbook and reference guide designed to prepare you to work with Microsoft® Works version 3.0 for Windows™ on an IBM or IBM-compatible PC. This book is intended for those who have a basic understanding of DOS and Windows 3.1.

Works for Windows consists of three applications—a word processor, a spreadsheet program, and a database program—that function together. The programs complement each other so you can perform tasks such as the preparation of form letters and mailing labels or the addition of a spreadsheet chart to a word processing document. Also included in Works is a communications program so that you can link yourself to other computers and various information services. In addition, Microsoft Draw and Microsoft WordArt, called applets (small applications), are included so that you can add graphics (pictures) and fancy text to your work.

This workbook is divided into one part for each of the three major applications and a final part to illustrate how the Works components integrate to become a comprehensive program. The fourth part also includes a discussion of the Works communications program. The workbook is further divided into chapters, each containing a discussion of new concepts, activities where those concepts are practiced, and On Your Own sessions that let you experiment with what you've learned.

The four parts of the book are:

Part I—The Word Processor

Part II—The Spreadsheet Program

Part III—The Database Program

Part IV—Making Works Work for You

Organization

Up and Running with Works 3.0 for Windows contains the following components:

- Chapter overviews and objectives

- Instructional notes for each topic

- Step-by-step references to accomplish each function

- Screen facsimiles

- Guided hands-on activities

- Unguided On Your Own exercises and case studies

- Index

Although *Up and Running with Works 3.0 for Windows* is comprehensive, it's *not* a user's manual. Refer to the *Microsoft Works User's Guide* for information not contained in this workbook.

NOTE: The best way to use this book is to do each part sequentially, step-by-step, since many activities build on concepts developed and files created in previous units. Similarly, most exercises build on each other. If you follow the steps to complete one exercise, you should be able to begin the next activity without additional preparation. **Do not save or close a document unless you are instructed to do so.** Work through the part on the word processor first. Several basic concepts that appear in all three programs are explained in detail there.

Conventions

- In the narrative text, nonalphabetic keys to be pressed are enclosed in brackets, for example, [F1], [Page Down], [Enter].

- In activities, keys to be pressed are shown as keycap symbols, for example, ENTER.

- Keys used in combination with the Control, Alt, or Shift keys are shown in the narrative text as [Shift] [F4] and in activities as SHIFT F4. The [Shift] key is held down while the [F4] key is pressed and released.

- Hands-on activities have numbered steps to distinguish them from reference material.

- Many activities have an On Your Own task to reinforce your knowledge. If you are unable to complete the task, ask your instructor for assistance.

- Text shown like the following is either text to be typed or an action to be performed by the student:

type **Second Qtr** *and press* ENTER

- Notes, Cautions, On Your Owns, Case Studies, Quick Checks, and Key Terms are identified by the following symbols in the margin:

Note	Caution
On Your Own	Case Study
Quick Check	Key Term

Student Diskette

The following files are found on your student diskette. While working through this book, you'll change several of these files. For this reason, you should make a copy of the original diskette and use it when working through the exercises.

ACME.WPS	INSTABS.WPS	REALRPT.WDB
ATLAS.WDB	INVEST.WKS	REALTYDB.WDB
ATLASPOP.WDB	LABLDATA.WDB	REGSALES.WKS
BLUSEDAN.WMF	LABOR.WKS	REGSALES.WPS
CHARTS.WKS	LABORF.WKS	SCHTAB.WPS
CHECK.WPS	MED.WPS	SCITY.WKS
COINS.WDB	MVANDCP.WPS	STAFF.WDB
COINS.WMF	MYCITYCA.WKS	STAFFRPT.WDB
COINSFO.WDB	MYCITYFO.WKS	TESTAVG.WDB
COPY.WKS	NLETTER.WPS	TMEMO.WPS
DISK35.WMF	OYOMLET.WPS	TRAIN.WPS
DISK525.WMF	PMTSTUDY.WKS	TRAVEL.WPS
EDIT.WPS	POSTER.WPS	TRUST.WPS
FINRPT.WPS	RANGES.WKS	

System Setup

The activities presented here assume this system configuration for each workstation:

- An IBM or IBM-compatible computer running Windows 3.1 and Works 3.0 for Windows. It's assumed that the Works software is installed in the C:\MSWORKS directory. This is the directory that the Works Setup uses unless instructed differently.

- A floppy disk drive designated as drive A: in which the student disk will be inserted. If another floppy disk drive is to be used for the student disk, that drive designator should be substituted in any activity that refers to drive A:.

- Access to a laser printer from each workstation. A dot matrix printer may also be used, but with reduced quality. General instructions for printing are supplied; however, they may require some modification depending on the printer used.

- A mouse input device. Keyboard equivalents for some mouse procedures are available, but a mouse is assumed to be the primary input device for all activities.

Acknowledgments

We would like to acknowledge the following individuals for making *Up and Running with Works 3.0 for Windows* possible: Ken Robertson who wrote the book; Chris Wolf who contributed additional material and tested the activities; Betsy Berlin who desktop-published the book; Lisa White who produced the book; and Carolyn Adler who conceived it.

We welcome all questions and comments from users of this workbook.

electronic learning facilitators, inc.
7910 Woodmont Avenue, Suite 630
Bethesda, Maryland 20814

Contents

CHAPTER 4

Formatting   51

CHAPTER 8
Editing and Formatting   145

CHAPTER 9
Functions and Features   165

CHAPTER 10
Charting 185

Part III
The Database Program 205

CHAPTER 11
Building a Database 207

CHAPTER 15

Communications 289

A First Look at Works

1

Overview

This book is designed for you, even if you're a computer novice. Works 3.0 for Windows contains all the basic elements of the three most important personal computer applications: a word processor, a spreadsheet, and a database. In addition, Works provides a communications program so you can use a modem to transmit your work to a distant computer or obtain data from another computer or an information service. These programs are designed with the beginner in mind and are simple to use yet so complete that Works may be all the software you'll need. All three programs use the Windows 3.1 interface. This means that every element common to the programs, and other Windows programs as well, are similar in operation. For example, if you want to save your work permanently on the hard disk, you'll do it the same way with each program. Thus, many Works basic functions need only be learned once.

Windows, and thus Works, uses a **GUI**, a graphical user interface, which means that you will work with icons on the screen rather than typing commands with the keyboard. Another convention used by Windows and Works is **WYSIWYG**—what you see is what you get. This means whatever you see on your screen will print (with minor exceptions). This way, you can visualize your final result before you print.

In this first chapter you'll be introduced to the way Works 3.0 looks as a Windows program. If you're already familiar with Windows 3.1, you can skim this chapter and go on to Chapter 2 after you've learned how to start Works 3.0 for Windows.

Objectives

- Start Works 3.0 for Windows
- Start the Works word processor
- Identify the parts of the window
- Use the mouse to select and drag
- Maximize, minimize, and restore a window
- Close Works

Getting Started

If Windows 3.1 and Works 3.0 for Windows have been properly installed on your computer, an icon representing Works should appear in a Microsoft Works for Windows group window. However, if someone has been working with your computer, you may find it placed within a different group. The Works icon is the one on the left in the figure below. If Works has not been installed, follow the instructions in *Installing Works on your computer* in the *Microsoft Works User's Guide*.

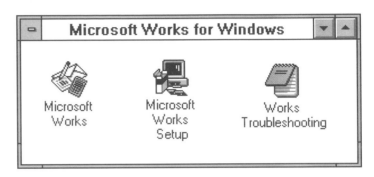

Using the Mouse

Windows is designed to be used primarily with a mouse but can also be used with a keyboard. Throughout this book, preference goes to mouse methods.

The mouse should lie on a smooth surface with the mouse cable facing away from you. For this reason, a mouse pad is a worthwhile investment. Perhaps the easiest way to control the mouse is to place your hand lightly on its base with your wrist resting on your desk or pad and your index finger lying lightly on the left mouse button. If you're left-handed, you can switch the right and left mouse buttons by opening the Control Panel and Mouse utility program in the Main group of the Windows Program Manager. As you move the mouse on your desk, the mouse pointer moves on the screen.

- You **point** to an item by moving the tip of the pointer onto the item.

- You **select** an item by pointing to it and then pressing and releasing the left mouse button. This is called **clicking**. Clicking will always mean using the left mouse button unless you're specifically told to **click right**. You'll know that you've successfully selected the item if it's highlighted.

- You **move** an object by pointing to it, pressing and holding down the left mouse button, and moving the pointer to the desired location. You release the button at the desired location. This is called **dragging**.

- You **open** a program by pointing to the item and clicking the left mouse button two times quickly: click-click. This is called **double-clicking**.

In your first activity you'll open Works 3.0 for Windows and start the word processor.

ACTIVITY 1.1

Starting Works 3.0 for Windows

1. Open Works.

    double-click the Microsoft Works icon

    Frequently there is more than one way to accomplish a task. You also could have opened Works by clicking the Works icon and pressing [Enter].

Welcome to Microsoft Works

For a guided tour of Microsoft Works and what you can do with Works, click this button or press T.   **Guided Tour of Works**

To start using Works now, click this button or press W.   **Start Works Now**

When you no longer want Works to start with this welcome screen, click this button or press S. The guided tour and other information can always be accessed from the Help menu.   **Skip Welcome Screen**

If Works has just been installed, you will see a welcome screen. From it you can start a tutorial program for a guided tour, or you can start the Works program. If you click the third choice, Skip Welcome Screen, the welcome will no longer appear when you start Works. Instead you will immediately see the *Startup* dialog box.

The *Startup* box contains two sets of buttons. Along the left are five buttons with the New & Recent Documents button appearing already pressed. This is the default choice. If you would like information about the four buttons, click Instructions. When you have finished reading the instructions click New & Recent Documents to make that choice active again. We will return to the other buttons later.

When the New & Recent Documents button has been chosen the *Startup* dialog box displays four additional buttons and a list box. Clicking one of these buttons will start the corresponding Works program. If you have already created files using one of the programs, their names will be displayed in the list box. You can open one of these files together with its Works program by double-clicking the file name. You'll have a chance to work with the *Startup* box buttons in the next chapter. Right now you'll do several activities to familiarize yourself with the Works window.

ACTIVITY 1.2

Closing the Startup Box

1. Close the *Startup* box.

    click Cancel in the upper right corner of the Startup *box*

    The Works 3.0 window is displayed without a document in place.

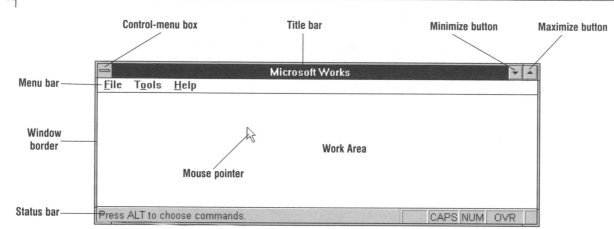

Notice the parts of the window in the above figure. The parts have the following functions:

Title Bar—Shows the name of the application: Microsoft Works. If a document is open, the document name will also be shown in the Title bar.

Control-Menu Box—On the left end of the Title bar is the Control-menu box. When selected this box provides a menu for sizing, moving, or closing the application window.

The Maximize and Minimize (Sizing) Buttons—The down arrow is called the **Minimize** button and is used to shrink a window to an icon. The up arrow is called the **Maximize** button and is used to enlarge a window to the screen. If a window already fills the screen, the Maximize button will be replaced by a two-headed arrow called the **Restore** button, which returns a window to an intermediate size.

Menu Bar—The Menu bar provides a selection of command menus.

Status Bar—The Status bar lies across the bottom and gives the status of commands and helpful hints. Check the Status bar if you aren't sure what to do next or if something goes wrong.

Work Area—When a Works program is active, the work area becomes a window used to enter text or data. Each Works program has its own window.

Window Borders—Each window has a border to define its perimeter. When a window isn't full size, you may drag a border or border corner to change the size of the window.

Take a few minutes to become familiar with the various window parts. In the next activity, you'll experiment with the mouse and the Works window.

ACTIVITY 1.3

Using the Mouse with the Works Window

1. Select a menu.

    click File in the Menu bar

    A pull-down menu of commands appears. You select a command by clicking it. Create New File and Open Existing File are commands that create a new file in one of the three programs or open an existing file. Works Wizards and Templates are commands to create files that are already partially finished. The commands Close, Save, and Save As are dimmed because as yet you have no file to close or save.

2. Click somewhere in the Work Area to escape from the menu (or press [Esc]).

    click in the Work Area

3. Minimize the Works program to an icon.

    click the Minimize button

    The Microsoft Works icon may now be hidden under the Program Manager or another application if several are running at once.

4. Return to the Works window.

    if the Microsoft Works icon is visible, double-click it

    if the icon isn't visible, minimize the Program Manager and any other applications until the icon appears, then double-click it

    or

    hold down the [Alt] key and press [Tab] repeatedly until the Microsoft Works name appears in a box at the center of the screen, then release the [Alt] key

5. Maximize the window.

    click the Maximize button

    After you click the Maximize button, it becomes the Restore button consisting of a two-headed arrow. When you click the Restore button to restore the window to an intermediate size, it again becomes the Maximize button.

ACTIVITY 1.4

Sizing the Works Window

1. Move the right window border.

    click the Restore button to restore the window to an intermediate size

    move the mouse pointer until it points at the right border of the Works window

    The pointer changes to a two-headed arrow that straddles the border.

    drag the border to the left across approximately one-third of the screen

2. Move the other borders.

    drag the left, bottom, and top borders until the window is a small square in the center of the screen

    Leave enough room for the menu to be displayed.

3. Maximize the window.

    click the Maximize button

4. Restore the window.

    click the Restore button

    Notice that the window is restored to the size it was before you maximized it.

    enlarge the restored window by dragging the corners

    You can drag a corner diagonally.

ACTIVITY 1.5

Quitting Works

1. Quit Works.

    from the menu select File, Exit Works

    Works is closed and you're returned to the Windows 3.1 Program Manager.

On Your Own

Try to repeat the activities in this chapter on your own.

- Start the Works program.

- Press the Cancel button.

- Minimize Works.

- Maximize Works.

- Restore Works.

- Change the size of the Works window; try dragging a corner.

- Quit the program (you can also quit Works by double-clicking the Control-menu box).

Quick Check

1. How do you start Works 3.0 for Windows?

2. Name the various parts of the window below.

Microsoft Works	▼ ▲
File Tools Help	

Press ALT to choose commands.   CAPS NUM OVR

3. How do you minimize a window?

4. What do you do if you can't find the Works icon after minimizing the program?

5. How do you size a window?

6. How do you exit Works?

Part I
The Word Processor

In This Section

- ❑ *Start the word processor*
- ❑ *Create, edit, format, and print a word processing document*
- ❑ *Create tables*
- ❑ *Customize the Works word processing window*
- ❑ *Add headers and footers to a document*
- ❑ *Proof a document*
- ❑ *Use applets, templates, and Wizards*

Word Processor Basics

2

Overview

In this chapter you will be introduced to the Works for Windows 3.0 word processing program and work with your first document. After learning about the word processing window, you'll create, edit, save, and print the document. These are the fundamental tasks associated with every document. Once you have mastered these essentials you can concentrate on the finer aspects of word processing.

Objectives

- Understand the principles of word processing
- Start the Works for Windows 3.0 word processor
- Identify the parts of the word processor window
- Create a simple document
- Save the document
- Print the document
- Close the Works word processor

For the Student New to Word Processing

If you've never used a word processor before, you need to know a few things about entering text. There are significant differences between a word processor and a typewriter.

- Do not press [Enter] at the end of each line. Use [Enter] only to start a new paragraph. The Works word processor will wrap, or move, a word that exceeds the right margin to the next line automatically. If you use [Enter] at the end of each line, the word processor will not be able to readjust the paragraph margins later if you add or delete text.

- Do not use [Spacebar] to move the **insertion point** (the blinking vertical line that shows where the next character will be typed) to a new location. Instead, use the four **arrow keys** or the mouse to move the insertion point. Use [Spacebar] only to insert spaces between words and sentences.

- Do not use [Spacebar] for indention or to line up text. Use [Tab] instead.

- To create a paragraph, move the insertion point to the place where the paragraph is to begin and press [Enter]. To combine paragraphs, move the insertion point to the left of the first character of the second paragraph and press [Backspace].

- If you make a mistake in typing, press [Backspace] to erase it. If you've made a mistake elsewhere in your text, use the arrow keys to move the insertion point immediately to the right of the error, then press [Backspace]. Type the correction. The text to the right of the insertion point will push aside to make room for the correction. If the line length changes, Works will automatically adjust the right margin.

If you are new to word processing you can also look forward to:

- On-screen editing, which allows you to correct errors and make changes before you print a document.

- Using **bold** and *italics* to emphasize words and phrases.

- The ability to save documents permanently on disk for future use.

- Four kinds of tabs that you set and move to align text in columns.

- Four kinds of paragraph alignment.

- A spelling checker and thesaurus to help with proofing.

- The use of charts and pictures in your documents.

The Works Word Processor Window

You have already seen that when you start Works for Windows 3.0, you are presented with a default startup screen offering four program options plus Cancel and Help. If you click the Word Processor button you will see a screen similar to the one shown on the next page.

Notice that now you have a *Document* window with its own Title bar in addition to the Microsoft Works window and Title bar. In this book we will use the term document to refer to the product you are creating with one of the three Works programs. Each document has its own window. (Later you will find that you can have more than one document open and displayed.) The document window also has a border that you can drag to change the size of the window, Maximize and Minimize buttons, and a Control-menu box. These features have similar functions to those you learned for the Works window.

The new parts of the document window:

Toolbar

Microsoft Works

File   Edit   View   Insert   Format   Tools   Window   Help

Times New Roman | 12 | B | I | U

Word1

End of paragraph mark

Document title bar

Ruler

End of document mark

I-beam pointer

Page mark

Scroll bars

Press ALT to choose commands.

CAPS | NUM

Pg 1/1

Word Processor

Document Title Bar—The name of the document is displayed in the Title bar. When a document is newly created, Works will name it DocumentX where X stands for the number of documents created during this Works session. Later, when you save the document, you will give it a name.

Ruler—The ruler is used to define tab stops, indents, and margins. If the ruler isn't showing in your document window, choose View, All Characters from the Works Menu bar.

Toolbar—The Toolbar contains a row of icons or buttons and text boxes that you can use to simplify choosing commands. If the Toolbar is not showing in your document window, choose View, Toolbar.

Scroll Bars—When a window contains more information than is visible inside the window borders, scroll bars will allow you to move horizontally or vertically through the window. Each scroll bar has an arrow at each end. In the word processor, you can move up or down a line of text by clicking the appropriate arrow. Each scroll bar also contains a scroll box. Clicking below the scroll box in the vertical scroll bar will move the window down one full screen. You can also drag the scroll box to an intermediate position. In a document of many pages, dragging the scroll box halfway down the scroll bar will take you to the middle of the document.

In the document window you will find several marks intended to help in editing the document:

Page Mark—A » symbol appears in the left margin to show the beginning of each page.

End of Document Mark—A horizontal line that shows the end of the document. No text can be placed below this mark.

Insertion Point—The position where the next character of text will be typed. The insertion point blinks so you can find it easily.

I-Beam Pointer—The pointer is used to change the position of the insertion point by clicking at a desired location within the text area.

End of Paragraph Mark—A ¶ symbol appears at the end of each paragraph. If the paragraph mark is not visible, choose View, All Characters from the Menu bar.

Your First Document

When you start the Works word processor, a new document will appear on screen with the insertion point already positioned at the top of the document ready for you to begin typing. If Works and the document window are not maximized when the program begins, click the Maximize button in the Works window and then the Maximize button in the document window.

If you haven't used a word processor before, take the time to watch how Works handles your typing. Pay particular attention to what happens as the typing approaches, then reaches, the right margin. In the next activity, press [Enter] only where you see the ¶ symbol.

Marks like ¶ are called non-printing symbols and are intended to let you see keystrokes that are not normally visible, making it easier for you to edit a document.

Other commonly used symbols:

- • space (should be one between each word)

- → tab

In the next activity you will type a short letter to an applicant for a job with the DSR Corporation. DSR is a mythical company that provides services in a number of fields. Its motto: "If you want it done real bad, we can give it to you that way."

Unlike a typewriter, when you type text with a word processor you can easily correct errors. This means you can speed up your typing without being overly concerned with mistakes. As you type you may realize that you have just pressed the wrong key. If you do, press [Backspace] to erase the mistake and continue. When you finish the letter you can go back and correct any errors that you missed as you typed.

Cue Cards

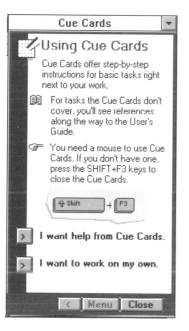

Cue Cards have been added to Works 3.0 to help the new user with step-by-step instructions. At the end of the chapter you will look at how Cue Cards can help when you're in a jam. Turn them off as a part of the next activity so you can work on your own.

ACTIVITY 2.1

Creating Your First Document

1. Start Works and go to the word processor.

    double-click the Works icon

    if the Welcome screen appears, click the Start Works Now button

    click the Word Processor button in the Startup *box*

2. Turn off the Cue Cards.

    click the button next to the words I want to work on my own

    click the button next to the words Close Cue Cards

Word Processor

3. Prepare the windows for your document.

    if the Works window is not maximized, click the program Maximize button

    if the Document window is not maximized, click the document Maximize button

    if you do not see the End of Paragraph mark, ¶ , choose View, All Characters

4. Type the letter on the next page. Type as fast as you like. Remember to press [Enter] only where you find a ¶ symbol. Your sentences may not wrap in the same place as shown in the text because of the different page margins or selected font. You will learn how to set margins later.

5. If you make errors, correct them using the arrow keys to move the insertion point to the right of the mistake and [Backspace] to erase it. Then type the correct text.

DSR Corporation¶
1236 Brighton Lane¶
Bethesda, MD 22003¶
¶
Ms. Shirley Reynolds¶
815 Mound Drive¶
Arlington, VA 22313¶
¶
Dear Ms. Reynolds:¶
¶
We have received your application for a position as
Administrative Assistant to the Chief Legal
Advisor. We appreciate your interest in DSR
Corporation, and we will give close attention to your
application.¶
¶
In order that we may have a better understanding
of your capabilities, we would like you to submit a
summary of your experience in using the personal
computer and computer applications. We are
particularly interested in whether you have used
word processing and spreadsheet programs and
have any knowledge of merge mailing. We will
continue consideration of your application on
receipt of your reply.¶
¶
Sincerely,¶
¶
¶
¶
¶
Wanda Thomas¶
Manager, Personnel¶
¶

Saving Your Work

So far, your document resides only in the temporary memory of the computer. An interruption of power would destroy all your work. The next step is to save your work permanently.

Your document has the temporary name [Word1]. When you save your work for the first time you must give the document a permanent name and choose a place for it on your hard disk or a diskette. Works uses dialog boxes whenever additional information is required to complete a command. The name must follow the DOS rules for file names. Use a maximum of eight characters without spaces. Works automatically supplies the .WPS file name extension. You'll save your work on the student diskette unless your instructor tells you differently. To save your work use the File, Save As command.

Before you begin the next activity, study the *Save As* dialog box below.

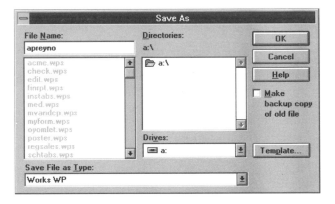

Any menu command with an ellipsis (**...**) following its name uses a dialog box for additional information. The *Save As* box illustrates several items that can appear in a dialog box.

List Box—A list box contains choices. The *Save As* dialog box above shows three list boxes, *Directories*, *Drives*, and *Save File as Type*. If a list box, for example, *Drives*, shows only one choice, click the box to see the remainder of the list. If the list is too long to fit in the box, a scroll bar appears. Click the down or up arrows to scroll through the list. Click your choice to select it. When all your choices have been made, click OK or press [Enter].

Combo Box—This box contains both a list box and a text box. You can either select an item from the list or type in a selection in the text box. File Name: is an example of combo box in the *Save As* dialog box.

Check Box—If you click on a check box, you make the option active. Click again and the option becomes inactive. An active option shows an X in the box. In the *Save As* dialog box, Make backup copy is an example of a check box.

ACTIVITY 2.2
Saving a File

1. Begin to save your work.

    choose File, Save As

    The *Save As* dialog box appears.

2. Select a drive.

    click inside the Drives *list box*

    A list of drives appears. You should have an A: and a C: drive, and you may have other drives as well.

    click the A: drive icon inside the list box

    The A: drive becomes the active drive. This step may take a few seconds. Under the word *Directories* at the top of the dialog box you will see **a:\.** This shows the drive and directory in which the file will be saved. The "\" stands for the root directory. If you get an error message regarding the drive, you may not have the diskette in place or the drive lever may be closed.

3. Give the file a name.

    click in the File Name *text box to the right of the temporary name*

    use [Backspace] to remove the name

    type **APREYNO** *in the text box (APREYNO for APplicationREYNOlds)*

4. Save the file and close the dialog box.

    choose OK or press [ENTER]

    You can either choose OK or press [Enter] because, if you notice, the border around the OK button is dark. This is called the default button. Any time you press [Enter] in a dialog box, it's equivalent to clicking the default button.

    The next time you save your file you can use the File, Save command because you have now named the file and selected a location (the A: drive) for it to be placed. If you want to save the file by another name or in a different location, again use the File, Save As command.

Word Processor

In addition to using the File, Save command from the menu, Works provides shortcut keys for frequently used commands. Since saving your work is a command you should use frequently (how frequently depends on how much unsaved work you're willing to risk), a shortcut key can save time. Shortcut keys are listed beside their commands in the command menus. The shortcut key for File, Save is [Ctrl] [S].

ACTIVITY 2.3

Saving Your Work with the Menu and Shortcut Key

1. Save your work with the menu.

    choose File, Save

    The Status bar records the progress of the save.

2. Save your work with a shortcut key.

    choose File

    press [ESC] *to remove the menu*

    press [CTRL] [S] *to save*

Printing

Always save your document prior to printing. That way any possible problems with the printer will not cause you to lose your work. Later you'll examine printing in more detail, but for now, you'll print your document by clicking the Print icon on the Toolbar. The Print icon is shown as a picture of a printer at the right end of the Toolbar.

ACTIVITY 2.4

Printing Your Document

1. Save your document.

    choose File, Save

2. Check to see that your printer is turned on and is on-line.

3. Print the document.

    click the Print icon

Works responds by displaying a box that reports APREYNO.WPS is being printed. If all goes well, the document will print within a few moments. If not, check again to make sure the printer is on-line.

Closing a Document

You should always save before closing a document. If you make any changes since the last time you saved and then try to close the document, Works will respond with a caution box asking if you want to *Save changes to: APREYNO.WPS?* Click the Yes button if you want to save the changes and the No button if you want to close the document without saving the changes. Click Cancel to return to the document screen.

ACTIVITY 2.5

Closing a Document

1. Save the document.

   choose File, Save

2. Close the document.

   choose File, Close

   You can also close a document by double-clicking the *document* Control-menu box. Be careful not to click the Works application Control-menu box unless you want to close Works 3.0.

Word Processor

On Your Own

Repeat the steps that you've learned to create, edit, save, and print the memo shown below. The → symbol means you are to press [Tab]. Save your work by the name WPMEMO. Close the document. Start by choosing File, Create New File and click the Word Processor button.

→ → → →   MEMO¶
¶
TO: → →   All Personnel¶
¶
FROM: → → Management¶
¶
SUBJECT: → DSR Company Picnic¶
¶
DATE: → → *Type in today's date*¶
¶
¶
The company picnic is scheduled for Saturday, July 1, starting at 1 p.m. and lasting until all the food is eaten. The location is, again, the old Dawson farm off Singleton Road. Your whole family is invited, and there will be games and prizes for young and old. See you on the 1st.¶
¶
¶
→ → →   *type your name here*¶
→ → →   Your President¶

Help

In this short chapter you have learned how to create, edit, save, and print a document. It is only natural that you may have forgotten just how to do each task. That, of course, will come with practice. Meanwhile, you may need additional help.

If you didn't have this book you might want to use the Works 3.0 on-screen tutorial. You can start the tutorial by clicking the yellow question mark at the right end of the Toolbar. The tutorial will give you an overview of many of the features of Works.

Sometimes help appears in unexpected places. You may already have noticed that if you point to one of the tools in the Toolbar for a moment a small yellow box will appear to tell you what that tool does.

Works also has an extensive help system for looking up forgotten commands and learning various tasks. You have access to this information through the Help menu or by pressing [F1]. But there are even quicker ways of getting specific help.

- If you need help while within a dialog box, press the Help button.

- If you need general information, choose the Help Index command in the Help menu.

In the next activity you will use the Help button in a dialog box to find information about the File, Save As command. Later, you will learn how to use Help to find information about other topics using the Search command.

ACTIVITY 2.6

Using the Help Button in a Dialog Box

1. Open the *Save As* dialog box.

   choose File, Save As

2. Get Help.

   click the Help button in the dialog box

   The Works for Windows Help window is like any other. You can scroll through it by using the scroll bar or change the size of the box by dragging the borders. Read the information about the Save As command.

   Notice that certain words in the information paragraphs have a dotted underline and are green on a color monitor. Clicking these words provides a definition of the term. Other relevant topics are listed at the bottom of the page.

3. Use Help for the definition of terms.

   click the word drive in the first information paragraph

4. Find Help about an associated topic.

   use the scroll bar to go to the bottom of the Help document

   click the topic Creating backup copies to protect your work

5. Cancel Help.

   double-click the Help Control-menu box

Word Processor

Using Cue Cards

While Help gives information about specific topics, Works Cue Cards give step-by-step instructions on how to carry out a task. The Cue Cards are designed to stay on top of the Works window so you can use them as you work.

To have Cue Cards displayed:

- Choose Help, Cue Cards. A check mark will be placed beside the command in the menu. Cue Cards will appear each time you create a document or open an existing document.

- Choose Help, Cue Cards a second time to turn off Cue Cards. The check mark will be removed from the menu.

ACTIVITY 2.7
Using Cue Card Instructions

1. Create a document.

   choose File, Create New File

   click the Word Processor button

2. Type a short sentence.

   type **Using Cue Cards for help with saving a document**

3. Start Cue Cards and find instruction on how to save.

   choose Help, Cue Cards

   read the information, then click the button beside I want help from Cue Cards

   read the topic choices in the Word Processor Menu *window*

   click the bottom button, Saving and printing

   in the next screen click Save your work

4. Follow the instructions to give the new file a name.

   read the Does the file you want to save have a name? *window*

   click No

read the next window and follow the two steps listed in the Saving your work for the first time *window*

name your file **CUETEST**

If the *Save As* dialog box covers the Cue Card, click in the Cue Card.

click Next in the Cue Card

read the final Cue Card window and carry out its instructions by clicking OK in the Save As *dialog box*

click Done in the Cue Card window

close the Cue Cards by clicking Close 2 times

Quick Check

1. Why should you press [Enter] at the end of paragraphs, but not at the end of every line of text?

2. How do you correct an error while typing?

3. How do you turn non-printing characters on or off?

4. What step should you take frequently to keep your work from being lost?

5. How often should you take this step?

6. What is the quick way to print a document?

7. How do you find information about a command that uses a dialog box?

8. How do you find step-by-step instructions about a specific task?

Editing with the Word Processor

Overview

In this chapter you'll learn additional techniques for editing text and moving around in a document. You'll also learn the important task of selecting (highlighting) text. You can already do almost anything with the Works word processor that you can do with a typewriter. When you finish this chapter you will be able to do many things that you can't do with a typewriter.

Objectives

- Open an existing document
- Select text for editing
- Navigate a document using the mouse and the keyboard
- Copy, move, and delete blocks of text
- Undo the last edit to recover from errors
- Find and replace text
- Open and work with multiple documents

Opening a Document

Before you can work with an existing document you must retrieve it from a diskette or your hard disk. Works calls this opening a document.

- Works takes a copy of the document from disk and places it in the memory of the computer. The document then appears on screen.
- Several documents can be open at one time.
- If you have more than one document open, you can easily switch from one to another or display them in separate windows at the same time.

Works makes it easy to open a document if it is one of the last four that have been opened. Choosing File from the Menu bar displays the File menu. At the bottom of the File menu is a list of the last four documents opened. The documents WPMEMO.WPS (if you did the On Your Own) and APREYNO.WPS should be at the top of the list unless other documents have been saved since you completed Chapter 2.

ACTIVITY 3.1

Opening a Document with the File List

1. Start the Works word processor. Open the File menu.

    choose File on the Menu bar

2. Find and open APREYNO.WPS from the file list.

    click APREYNO.WPS in the file list

    If you did not do the activity in the previous chapter, the file name will not appear in the file list.

3. When the document appears on screen, move to the address lines and replace *Arlington* with *Alexandria*.

    click to the right of the word Arlington, *then use* [←BACKSPACE] *to delete the word*

    type **Alexandria**

4. Save the document.

    choose File, Save or press the shortcut keys [CTRL] [S]

5. Close the document.

    choose File, Close

    Another way to close a document is to double-click the document (not the Works program) Control-menu box. A third way is to press [Ctrl] [F4].

Open an Existing File with the Menu

Frequently, the document you want to open isn't in the File list. In this case you must open the document using the File, Open Existing File command and the *Open* dialog box.

*   The *Open* dialog box lists all the files in the current directory that have the extensions .WPS (word processor documents), .WKS (spreadsheets), and .WDB (database files).

*   If the document you want is listed in the *File Name* box, you can double-click the file name, or you can choose the file name and then press [Enter] or click the OK button. You may have to scroll through the list in the *File Name* box to find your file.

- If the file is in a different directory or on another disk, you must use the *Directories* and *Drives* list boxes to find and open the file.

- The current drive is shown in the *Drives* box. To change drives, choose the current drive to view the drive list, then choose the desired drive.

- The current directory is shown in the *Directories* box with the current directory highlighted. To change directories, double-click the desired directory. If the directory you want is not shown, double-click the parent directory at the top of the list to move to the directory one level above the current one. Then double-click the desired directory.

- If you know the complete path and name of the file, you can type it in the *File Name* text box and press [Enter].

ACTIVITY 3.2

Opening a Document with File, Open

1. Open a document with a command.

   choose File, Open Existing File

2. Open the file EDIT.WPS from the student diskette.

   click the Drives *list box*

   choose A: from the list of drives (or choose the drive containing the Works documents)

   double-click the file name EDIT.WPS to open the document

Saving a Document with a Different Name

Sometimes it's a good idea to make a copy of a document with a different name. Then, if you make a serious mistake, one from which you're unable to recover, you can retrieve another copy of the original document from disk. Saving a file with a new name closes the original file and makes the new copy active.

ACTIVITY 3.3

Saving a Copy of a Document

1. Open the File, *Save As* dialog box.

    choose File, Save As

2. Save the document with a different name.

    type **MYEDIT** *in the* File Name *text box*

    click OK

    The name in the document Title bar changes to MYEDIT.WPS. If a document by that name already exists you will be asked if you want to overwrite it. Answer Yes.

Selecting Text

Selecting text is one of the most important tasks in word processing. It means choosing the boundaries of a block of text or a graphic. Once the text or graphic is selected, you can do something with the entire block. For example, you might select text that you wanted to:

- Delete

- Move

- Copy

- Make **bold** or *italic* or <u>underline</u>

- Indent

Selected text is highlighted (shown in reverse video like the sentence in the figure below). You can select with either the keyboard or mouse. Works offers several choices with each.

```
Microsoft Works - [EDIT.WPS]
 File  Edit  View  Insert  Format  Tools  Window  Help
Times New Roman   12   B / U

                    The Future Arrives

     Have you ever tried to type a long letter without making a single mistake? An article
that looked clean and bright and perfect? If you have, unless you are an unusually careful
and competent typist, you found yourself either going very slowly or starting over, and
over, and over. Have you ever typed a long and spotless report only to find that the boss
wanted to make numerous additions, corrections, and deletions? Wouldn't it be nice if you
had a sort of electronic whiteout that would allow you to correct typing mistakes, to make
additions, corrections, and deletions without all the misery of starting over?

Page 1
Press ALT to choose commands.                      CAPS NUM        Pg 1/1
```

Word Processor

Selecting with the Keyboard

To select text with the keyboard, first use the arrow keys to move the insertion point to the beginning of the text to be selected.

- While holding down [Shift], use the arrow keys to move the insertion point to the end of the text to be selected. As you do, the text becomes highlighted. You can move left, right, up, or down. When the desired text has been highlighted, release [Shift].

- To change a highlighted selection, again hold down [Shift] and use the arrow keys.

- After the text is selected, pressing an arrow key without [Shift] will deselect the text.

ACTIVITY 3.4

Selecting from the Keyboard with the [Shift] Key

1. Select text by holding down [Shift] and using the right or left arrow keys.

   move the insertion point to the left of the word Have *(the first word of the first paragraph)*

   hold down **SHIFT** *and press* **→** *to move to the end of the sentence, then release* **SHIFT**

2. Undo the selection.

    press any arrow key

3. Select an entire paragraph.

    move the insertion point to the left of the word Have

    hold down **SHIFT** *and press* ↓ *to move the insertion point to the last line of the paragraph*

    hold down **SHIFT** *and press* → *to move to the end of the paragraph*

    press any arrow key to deselect the text

Selecting with the Mouse

It's often faster to select text with the mouse. You can do so in a variety of ways.

Dragging—You can select text with the mouse by dragging the pointer over the text to be selected. If the selection is larger than a single screen, the screen will scroll as you drag the mouse.

Clicking—To select a single word, move the pointer to the word and double-click. To select a single sentence, hold down [Ctrl] and click within the sentence.

Using the [Shift] Key—Use the mouse to move the insertion point to the beginning of the text. Move the pointer to the end of the text, hold down [Shift], and click.

Using the Selection Bar—The Selection bar is a narrow vertical strip along the left margin. When the mouse pointer is in the Selection bar, its shape changes from an I-beam to an arrow pointing up and to the right. You can select text by dragging the mouse pointer up or down along the Selection bar. Alternatively, you can:

*   Select a single line by clicking next to it in the Selection bar.

*   Select a paragraph by double-clicking next to it in the Selection bar.

*   Select the whole document by holding down the [Ctrl] key and clicking in the Selection bar.

Deselecting

Deselect text by clicking anywhere in the text area.

ACTIVITY 3.5

Dragging and Clicking

1. Make MYEDIT.WPS active and select the second paragraph.

   move the mouse I-beam pointer to the start of the second paragraph

   drag the pointer to the end of the paragraph

   If you drag too far to the right, the text may scroll off the screen. Drag back to the left to return to the left margin.

2. Deselect the text.

   click somewhere in the text area to deselect the text

3. Select a word of your choice.

   double-click within the word

4. Select a sentence of your choice.

   hold down `CTRL` *and click within the sentence*

ACTIVITY 3.6

Selecting with the Mouse and [Shift] Key

1. Select text with the mouse and the [Shift] key.

   click the I-beam pointer at the beginning of the second paragraph

   move (not drag) the I-beam pointer to the end of the paragraph

   hold down `SHIFT` *and click*

ACTIVITY 3.7

Using the Mouse and the Selection Bar

1. Select text with the mouse and the Selection bar.

   move the mouse pointer into the Selection bar

   move the arrow-shaped pointer beside the second line of the second paragraph

   click to select the line

2. Select a paragraph, then the entire document.

    move the pointer into the Selection bar beside the first paragraph

    double-click to select the paragraph

    hold down CTRL *and click in the Selection bar to select the entire document*

3. Deselect the document.

    move the mouse pointer into the text area and click to deselect

Help with Selecting

By now you can see there are many ways of selecting text, and the one you use in a particular situation depends on the text you want to select and whether you would prefer to use the mouse or the keyboard. You should learn to use both methods. Use Help for a ready reference of selection methods while you learn.

ACTIVITY 3.8

Making a Reference Guide Using Help

1. Searching through Help.

    choose Help, Search

2. Find help for Highlighting.

    type **high** *in the text box*

    As you type, Help moves alphabetically to the nearest topic. By the time you have typed *high*, the highlighting topics will have appeared. You may want to maximize the Help window so you have convenient use of the scroll bars.

    use the scroll bar to move down to highlighting: in word processor *in the list box and click it*

    click Show Topics

    click Highlighting in the Word Processor *in the* Topics *box*

    click Go To

3. Read and print the topic.

    choose File, Print Topic

    Note that a list of associated topics appears at the bottom of the Help screen. By moving to and then printing appropriate topics, you can make a small reference guide to help you learn and remember Works techniques.

4. Print an associated topic.

    click Keys for highlighting Word Processor information *in the list at the bottom of the Help screen.*

    chose File, Print Topic

    chose File, Exit to close Help

Clear and Undo

Erasing text with the [Backspace] key works well for a few characters, but erasing larger blocks of text becomes cumbersome. For large blocks you can clear or cut selected text.

*   To **clear**, first mark the block to be erased by selecting the text. Then press [Delete] in the block of keys above the arrow keys, or choose Edit, Clear.

*   Text deleted in this way is lost unless the next thing you do is **Undo** the deletion with the Edit, Undo command. The keyboard equivalent is [Alt] [Backspace]. Undo only undoes the most recent action.

You may undo (reverse) the most recent command or deletion with Undo.

*   If you make a mistake, choose Edit, Undo or press [Alt] [Backspace], **before performing any other action**.

*   Undo works with other actions as well, reversing the consequences of a previous command. Some commands, however, such as File, Save, *cannot* be undone.

ACTIVITY 3.9

Clearing and Undoing

1. Clear the document title.

    select the document title, The Future Arrives

    press **DEL**

2. Undo the deletion.

    choose Edit, Undo Editing

    The title is returned. The name of the Edit, Undo command changes to suit the action to be undone.

3. Clear the document title and type new text.

    select the document title

    choose Edit, Clear

    type **Gone Forever** *and press* [ENTER]

4. Try to get back the original title with Undo.

    choose Edit, Undo Editing

    The new title, *Gone Forever*, disappears. The old title does not reappear. The last action you performed was to type the words *Gone Forever* and this is the action that the Undo command undoes. You can only undo the most previous action or command.

5. Replace the text.

    type **The Future Arrives** *and press* [ENTER]

6. Close the document only if you do not intend to do the On Your Own exercise.

On Your Own

1. Make the document MYEDIT.WPS active if it isn't already (perform the necessary steps for MYEDIT.WPS to appear on screen in the word processor window). Turn on the non-printing symbols (View, All Characters).

2. Review the ways you may select text. Practice selecting using the keyboard, the mouse, and the mouse with the Selection bar. Try using the [F8] key to see if you like it. Highlight the whole document. Turn the [F8] extend function off by pressing the [Esc] key.

3. Delete selected text from MYEDIT.WPS—a word, a sentence, and a paragraph.

4. What happens if you delete a paragraph but do not delete the ¶ mark at the end of the paragraph? What happens if you select and delete the ¶ mark only? How do you put things back the way they were?

   The paragraph mark will cause an extra line in the text. If you delete a paragraph mark by mistake, the paragraph will be joined to the one following. To put things back, press [Enter] or choose Edit, Undo Editing.

5. Select and delete a sentence. Undo the deletion. When you delete a sentence, should you include the space at the end?

   Yes, otherwise there will be two spaces between sentences.

6. Close MYEDIT.WPS and do not save the changes. Choose File, Close, then answer No to the question *Save changes to: MYEDIT.WPS* by clicking the No button.

7. Use Help to find out about the Undo command. Close the Help window when you finish by double-clicking its Control-menu box. Close any other files that may be open.

Moving Around in Long Documents

Moving through a document with the arrow keys is not very practical. Instead, Works has a number of keyboard and mouse procedures that you may use to quickly move to a desired location within a document. Works even has special Go To commands.

While you're moving you can find your current page location in a document by referring to the far right block of the Status bar. There you're shown the current page followed by a slash and the number of pages in the document. You can also look at the left end of the horizontal scroll bar where the page number appears between two sets of buttons.

Moving with the Keyboard

Here are some of the keys for moving around in a document and their effects.

Key	Effect
[End]	moves to the end of the line
[Home]	moves to the beginning of the line
[Page Up]	moves up one screen
[Page Down]	moves down one screen
[Ctrl] [Page Up]	moves to the top of the document window
[Ctrl] [Page Down]	moves to the bottom of the document window
[Ctrl] [Home]	moves to the beginning of the document
[Ctrl] [End]	moves to the end of the document
[F5]	moves to a chosen page or bookmark

Moving with the Mouse

You can use the mouse and vertical scroll bar to move through a document. You can also use the four buttons at the left end of the horizontal scroll bar.

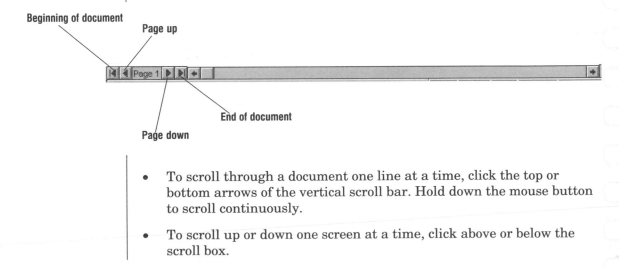

Beginning of document

Page up

Page 1

End of document

Page down

- To scroll through a document one line at a time, click the top or bottom arrows of the vertical scroll bar. Hold down the mouse button to scroll continuously.

- To scroll up or down one screen at a time, click above or below the scroll box.

- To scroll to a specific location in the document, drag the scroll box to the corresponding position in the scroll bar. For example, if you want to go to the middle of the document, drag the scroll box to the middle of the scroll bar. Dragging the scroll box to the bottom will take you to the end of the document.

- Click on the buttons in the horizontal scroll bar marked |< and >| to move to the beginning or end of the document. Click the < and > buttons to move up or down a page.

ACTIVITY 3.10

Moving Around in a Document

1. Open the document TRUST.WPS from the student diskette.

    click Open an Existing Document in the Startup *dialog box*

    double-click TRUST.WPS in the File Name *list box*

2. Move to the end of the document.

    press CTRL END

3. Move to the beginning of the document.

    press CTRL HOME

4. Move to the end.

    click the End of Document button in the horizontal scroll bar

5. Move to the beginning.

    click the Beginning of Document button in the horizontal scroll bar

6. Go to page 8.

    press F5

    type **8** *in the* Go To *text box and press* ENTER

    Look between the buttons on the horizontal scroll bar to verify that you are on page 8.

7. Leave the document open for the On Your Own and the next activity.

Word Processor

NOTE: There is a difference between moving around with the keyboard and moving around with the mouse. When you move with the keyboard, the insertion point moves to the new location. When you scroll through the document, the insertion point remains at its previous location until you click in the text at the new location.

On Your Own

1. Experiment with the other key combinations to move around within the document.

2. Experiment with using the vertical scroll bar. Click above the scroll box. How far did you move? Did the insertion point move? Click the page up or page down buttons in the horizontal scroll bar. How far did you move? Did the insertion point move?

   A screen. No. A page. Yes.

3. Go to page 11 using the Go To command, [F5], or by choosing Edit, Go To.

4. Leave the document TRUST.WPS open for the next activity.

Bookmarks

The Go To command also works with bookmarks. You can give any location in your document a bookmark name with the Insert, Bookmark Name command and then go there later with the Edit, Go To command. For example, a bookmark is a good way to mark where you stopped editing when you went to lunch. If you want to move a bookmark, delete the name, move to the new location, then reinsert the name.

ACTIVITY 3.11

Setting and Using Bookmarks

1. Make sure that TRUST.WPS is the active document.

2. Set a bookmark.

   move through the document to page 4, to the paragraph Distributions Upon Both Settlor's Deaths

   move the insertion point to the left of the word Distributions

   choose Insert, Bookmark Name

   in the Name *box type* **dist** *(you may use upper or lower case)*

   click OK

3. Set a second bookmark.

    move to page 7 to the heading titled Incapacity

    choose Insert, Bookmark Name and type **incap** *in the* Name *box*

    click OK or press ENTER

    Notice that the name of the first bookmark is now displayed in the *Names* list box.

    click the Top of Document button in the horizontal scroll bar

4. Find a bookmark.

    choose Edit, Go To

    double-click the bookmark name dist *to go the topic* Distributions Upon Both Settlor's Deaths

5. Go to the bookmark name *incap*.

6. Close the document TRUST.WPS without saving the changes.

Cut, Paste, Copy, and the Clipboard

In Works, you use cutting, copying, and pasting to move or copy text.

*   **Cut**—Cutting erases selected text from the screen, but unlike text that has been cleared (deleted), text that is Cut is placed on the Windows Clipboard where it's retained for future use. To cut text, first select the text, then choose Edit, Cut, or press [Ctrl] [X].

*   **Copy**—Copy leaves the selected text on the screen but moves a copy to the Clipboard. To copy text, first select the text, then choose Edit, Copy, or press [Ctrl] [C].

*   **Clipboard**—The Clipboard is for temporary storage. It can hold text, spreadsheet cells, graphics, and other objects, but *it only holds the last selection that was cut or copied*. Any new item placed in the Clipboard replaces previous material.

*   **Paste**—Once text has been cut from a document it's available to be pasted back. Not only may the text be pasted into active documents, but it may be pasted into another document or into any other application that supports the Clipboard. To paste, choose Edit, Paste, or press [Ctrl] [V].

- Cutting and pasting are sometimes called moving. The item is taken from one location and placed in another.

- Pasting doesn't remove the selection from the Clipboard; it only pastes a copy. You can paste the material over and over again.

ACTIVITY 3.12

Cut, Copy, and Paste

1. Open the file MED.WPS from the student diskette.

   click Open an Existing Document in the Startup *dialog box*

   double-click MED.WPS in the File Name *list box*

2. Cut and paste.

   select paragraph 3.(a) of the document by double-clicking beside it in the Selection bar

   choose Edit, Cut

   move the insertion point below paragraph 3.(b), just to the left of the « (the mark that appears between paragraphs)

   choose Edit, Paste to paste paragraph 3.(a) and reverse the order of the paragraphs

3. Put the paragraphs back in their original order.

   It helps to have the non-printing characters showing so you can include everything that belongs to the paragraph.

4. Copy the document title to the end of the document.

   select the document title, MEDICAL CARE REIMBURSEMENT PLAN

   choose Edit, Copy

   press [CTRL] [END] *to move to the end of the document*

   choose Edit, Paste

   move to the top of the document

   Note that the title is now at both the beginning and the end of the document.

5. Leave the document open for the next activity.

Drag and Drop

A quicker method than cutting and pasting has been added to Works 3.0. Called **drag and drop**, it allows you to select text and move it to a new location.

First select the text that is to be moved or copied.

- Move the mouse pointer into the selected text. The pointer becomes an arrow with the word DRAG beneath it.

- Drag the text to the new location. The word DRAG becomes MOVE. The position where the text will be inserted is shown by a vertical cursor.

- When the vertical cursor is positioned where you want, release the mouse button to move the text to its new location.

- If the [Ctrl] key is held down as the text is dragged, the mouse pointer shows the word COPY, and the text is copied to the new location.

- Drag and drop works best when moving or copying text within a single window. If you try to drag beyond the boundary of a window you may find that the document scrolls too fast to find your destination. Use cut and paste in such cases.

Word Processor

ACTIVITY 3.13

Dragging and Dropping Text

1. Be sure MED.WPS is the active document.

2. Move text by dragging.

    select paragraph 3.(a) of the document by double-clicking beside it in the Selection bar

    move the mouse pointer into the selected paragraph so it becomes an arrow with the word DRAG

drag the pointer below paragraph 3.(b), just to the left of the « (the mark that appears between paragraphs)

release the mouse button to move the paragraph

3. Use drag and drop to put the paragraphs back in their original order.

4. Close MED.WPS and do not save the changes.

On Your Own

1. Open the document MVANDCP.WPS from the student diskette.

2. The numbered subheadings in the three sections are in the wrong order. Put them in the correct order. Hint: Look carefully, you may be able to move more than one paragraph at a time.

3. The three sections are in the wrong order. Put them in the correct order.

4. Close MVANDCP.WPS without saving.

5. Close any additional documents that remain open before going on.

Finding and Replacing

You may find all occurrences of a word, phrase, or group of characters. If you choose, you may selectively replace the text with another word, phrase, or group of characters. You may limit the search to whole words, so that finding *he* will not find *she* and *her* as well. You may also find and replace non-printing characters.

```
┌─────────────────────────────────────────────────┐
│ ▬                    Find                        │
├─────────────────────────────────────────────────┤
│                                                  │
│  Fi̲nd What:  │doe                    │ ┌──────────┐ │
│                                       │Find Next│ │
│                                        └──────────┘ │
│  ☒ Match W̲hole Word Only              ┌──────────┐ │
│  ☐ Match C̲ase                         │ Cancel  │ │
│                                        └──────────┘ │
│                                        ┌──────────┐ │
│                                        │  Help   │ │
│                                        └──────────┘ │
└─────────────────────────────────────────────────┘
```

•   The text typed into the *Find What* text box may consist of text or non-printing characters.

•   Find and Replace starts from the insertion point and moves through the document, or through selected text. When finished, Works tells you how many replacements were made.

•   If you mark Match Whole Word Only, Works will not find the text if it is embedded within another word or phrase.

- If you mark Match Case, only text matching in case and content will be found. If you look for the word *Reed*, you'll find *Reed* but not *reed*.

- You can also look for non-printing characters. To find a tab, type **^t** in the *Find What* box. **The caret (^) character ([Shift] [6]) does not symbolize the [Ctrl] key.** You can also use the wild card character *?*: *Ju??* will find both *June* and *July*. Some other non-printing characters are:

^p	paragraph mark	^d	page break
^t	tab mark	^n	end of line mark

ACTIVITY 3.14

Finding Text

1. Open the document CHECK.WPS from the student diskette.

2. Start Find at the top of the document.

   press **[CTRL] [HOME]**

3. Open the *Find* dialog box and type a word to find.

   choose Edit, Find

   type **premiums** *in the* Find What *text box*

   be sure the Match Case check box is clear

   click the Find Next button

   click Cancel to close the dialog box

4. Repeat steps 2 and 3 with the Match Case check box marked.

   Did it find the same occurrence of the word?

5. Repeat a find.

   press **[CTRL] [HOME]** *to go to the top of the document*

   choose Edit, Find

   type **trust** *in the* Find What *text box and clear both the Match Case and Match Whole Word check boxes*

Word Processor

click the Find Next button

click Cancel to close the dialog box

press [F7] *to search for the next occurrence of the word*

continue pressing [F7] *until you reach the bottom of the document*
(or get tired of pressing [F7] *)*

Activity 3.15

Replacing Text and Non-Printing Characters

1. Be sure that CHECK.WPS is the active document.

2. Replace one phrase with another.

   go to the top of the document

   choose Edit, Replace

   type **John Doe** *in the* Find What *text box*

   type **Ralph Emerson** *in the* Replace With *text box*

   The replacement will be case sensitive. Type the text exactly as you want it to appear in the document.

   click the Replace All button

   read the number of replacements in the Status bar

   click the Close button

3. Replace the non-printing paragraph mark with a visible symbol.

   hide the non-printing characters

   press [CTRL][HOME] *to go to the top of the document*

   choose Edit, Replace

   type **^p** *in the* Find What *box and type* **@ @** *in the* Replace With *box* *click the Replace All button*

click the Close button and view the document

4. Close this and any other documents that may be open and do not save the changes.

Working with More than One Document

Any documents that you open will remain open rather than being replaced by succeeding documents. The documents will remain open until you close them or quit Works. You can use the Window menu to make the document that you want to work with active. At the bottom of the Window menu you will find a list of currently opened documents. The active document has a check mark beside its name.

You can also display more than one document at a time using the Window, Cascade and Window, Tile commands. When more than one document window is displayed you can move from one to another by clicking in the window you want to be active, or by pressing [Ctrl] [F6].

ACTIVITY 3.16
Using the Window Command

1. Close any open documents, then open two existing documents.

   open EDIT.WPS from the student diskette

   open TRUST.WPS from the student diskette

2. Make EDIT.WPS the active document.

   choose Window from the menu

   click EDIT.WPS in the file list

3. Display both documents.

   choose Window, Tile

   press **CTRL** **F6** *to jump to the other window*

   close both documents

Case Study

In this first case study you'll prepare a brief training memo. You've decided to combine parts of two existing documents with appropriate additions and deletions. When the memo is completed, you'll save it by a new name and print the document.

The two documents you will use are TMEMO.WPS and TRAIN.WPS.

1. Open the two documents from the student diskette.

2. Make TMEMO.WPS the active document.

3. Delete the paragraph about the Feb. 4 meeting.

4. At the location where you deleted the paragraph type:

   These program codes may be different from the ones you are familiar with. If you have any questions, please call me.

5. Make TRAIN.WPS the active document.

6. Go to the second page of TRAIN.WPS to the list of Program Codes.

7. Copy the list, including the headings, to the Clipboard.

8. Make TMEMO.WPS the active document and go to the bottom of the document.

9. Paste the list of Program Codes (from the Clipboard) into TMEMO.WPS.

10. Some of the codes will be out of order. Put the list in proper numerical order.

11. Move to the bottom of the document. Type your name, and on the line below, type **Training Office**. Save the document with the name MYTMEMO.WPS.

12. Print and close MYTMEMO.WPS.

13. Close any remaining documents. Do not save any changes.

Quick Check

Verify your answers to the questions below by carrying out the steps in Works where appropriate.

1. How do you open a document?

2. What is the purpose of selecting text?

3. What are some ways to select text using the keyboard?

4. Using the mouse, how do you select:

    a. A word?

    b. A paragraph?

    c. The entire document?

5. What's the purpose of the Undo command?

Word Processor

6. How do you move to the end of the document using the keyboard? the mouse?

7. What key or command lets you move to a specific page?

8. What is the difference between cut and copy?

9. List the steps required to move a paragraph from page 3 to page 16.

10. How could you count the number of paragraphs in a document. Hint: Replace all paragraph marks (^p) with paragraph marks (^p).

Formatting

Overview

The appearance of your finished document often has as much impact as what you have to say. A report becomes more readable and usable if headings are clearly marked, important points are numbered or bulleted, and paragraphs are set off by first-line indents or additional space between paragraphs. The character size of the general text should make it easy to read, and words and phrases intended to catch the eye might be *italic* or **bold**. Pages should use margins appropriate to the text, narrow for draft and wider for the finished document. Spacing might be double for draft and single spaced for the finished work. All of this is called formatting, changing the appearance of a document without changing the actual content, and it is an important part of document preparation.

Objectives

- Customize the Works word processor window for ease of formatting

- Customize the Toolbar with icons you use most

- Apply formatting to text

- Apply **bold**, *italic*, superscript and subscript, ~~strikethrough~~, underline, and other types of character formatting

- Use fonts to make your work more readable and more exciting

- Indent a paragraph from either or both margins and use a hanging indent

- Set line spacing to one, two, three lines, or to any value in between.

- Set the margins for a document

- Add a border around a paragraph

Customizing the Word Processor Window

At the top of the word processor window, just below the Menu bar is the Toolbar. At the top of each document window you will find the Ruler. You can show the Toolbar and Ruler or you can hide them to allow more text area. You can also show or hide non-printing characters. If an option is active, you will see a check mark beside the name of the option in the View menu. In the next activity you will change these options.

ACTIVITY 4.1

Changing the Show Options

1. Create a new document with the Works word processor. Maximize the windows.

2. Hide the Toolbar and Ruler.

   choose View, Toolbar

   choose View, Ruler

3. Show the Toolbar and Ruler.

   choose View, Toolbar

   choose View, Ruler

4. Restore the document window.

   click the document Restore button

   Notice that the Ruler is a part of the document window and the Toolbar is a part of the Works application window.

   click the document Maximize button

Other Screen Options

From the Tools menu you may also change the Works units of measurement for the Ruler and choose options for the word processor.

Options

Units
- ⦿ **I**nches
- ○ **C**entimeters
- ○ **P**ica
- ○ Poin**t**s
- ○ **M**illimeters

When starting Works
- ☐ **U**se saved workspace

In Word Processor
- ☐ O**v**ertype
- ☒ **T**yping replaces selection
- ☒ **A**utomatic word selection

[**OK**]
[**Cancel**]
[**H**elp]

Speller:
[American English ▼]

Spreadsheet and Database
Default num**b**er of decimals: [2]

- ☒ Sho**w** status bar
- ☒ Use **3**-D dialogs
- ☒ D**r**ag and drop
- ☒ **H**elpful mouse pointers
- ☐ Printer's envelope feeder is installed

Communications

Dial type
- ⦿ To**n**e
- ○ P**u**lse

Modem port:
[COM1 - Available ▼]

Send mail as
- ○ T**e**xt
- ⦿ **D**ocument

Units—The units of measure are shown in the Ruler and used for margins and indents. There are 2.54 centimeters, 72 points, or 6 picas to the inch.

Use Saved Workspace—When starting works, check this box to have Works open specific documents and display a preferred window arrangement each time you start the program. Arrange the documents and windows the way you want. Then choose the File, Save Workspace command to save the workspace. Use Show Startup Dialog to show or hide the Startup dialog box that appears each time you start Works.

Show Status Bar—Check this box if you want to have the Status bar showing at the bottom of the Works window.

Use 3-D Dialogs—The 3-D dialog boxes may be more attractive, but you might prefer to turn this feature off to make the text more readable.

Drag and Drop—If you wish, you may turn off the Drag and drop feature used to move and copy text.

Helpful Mouse Pointers—With the Helpful mouse pointers turned on, the mouse pointer includes directions on what you can do. For example, the pointer includes the word DRAG when pointing to selected text.

Overtype—When the overtype option is active, typing will replace existing text rather than push it aside.

Typing Replaces Selection—If text has been selected prior to typing, the selection in its entirety will be replaced by the newly typed text.

CAUTION: This option can be disconcerting. For example, if you have selected the entire document all the text will disappear when you press an alphabetic key.

Automatic Word Selection—This option automatically highlights entire words as you select text by dragging.

The remainder of the options deal with spreadsheets, databases, and communications. These options will be described in later chapters.

ACTIVITY 4.2

Saving Your Workspace

1. Close any documents that may be open, then open the file TRAVEL.WPS from the student diskette.

2. Maximize Works, then Restore and size the document window.

    click the Works, Maximize button (if the application is not already maximized)

    click the Restore button in the document window (if not already restored)

    drag the document window borders to leave one-half inch of space around the window

3. Save the Workspace.

    choose File, Save Workspace

4. Set the option.

    choose Tools, Options

    mark the Use saved workspace check box in the When starting Works area

5. Quit Works.

    choose File, Exit Works

6. Restart Works.

    double-click the Works icon in the File Manager

    The Works word processor starts with the saved workspace displayed.

7. Turn off the option.

    choose Tools, Options

    clear the Use saved workspace check box

8. Close the document and do not save the changes.

Character Formatting

It's easy to apply character formatting in Works. Simply select (highlight) the text and apply the format. Selecting is done in the same way you selected text for deleting, moving, or copying, and you can use any of the several methods that you learned then.

- As little as a single character may be formatted, or as much as an entire document.

- Once the text is selected, you may also use one of several methods to apply the character format.

- You can use the Format, Font and Style command; you can click the Bold, Italic or Underline icons on the Toolbar; or you can use a shortcut key.

The Toolbar

- Use the Toolbar to apply **bold**, *italic*, or <u>underline</u>. Select the text, then click the appropriate icon. When the formatting has been applied, the icon appears to have been pushed in.

- To apply more than one format, click each desired character formatting icon in turn.

- If different parts of selected text have different character formats, the icons will appear in reverse.

- To remove formatting, select the text and click the icon until the text is restored to its deselected position. You may have to click more than once.

ACTIVITY 4.3

Bold, Italic, and Underline with the Toolbar

1. Open the TRAVEL.WPS document and maximize the window.

2. Select text for formatting.

   select the heading DSR CORPORATION

3. Apply bold formatting to the selection.

   click the Bold icon on the Toolbar

   Note the appearance of the Bold icon.

4. Deselect the heading.

    click somewhere in the text area

5. Remove the bold formatting from the heading.

    select the bold heading

    click the Bold icon

    Again note the appearance of the Bold icon.

6. Leave the document open for the next activity.

Shortcut Keys

If you've been using the keyboard to select text, you may also want to use it to apply character formatting. You can do this using the [Ctrl] key together with an alphabetic key. The character formatting shortcut keys:

bold	[Ctrl] [B]	italic	[Ctrl] [I]
subscript	[Ctrl] [=]	subscript	[Ctrl] [Shift] [=]
underline	[Ctrl] [U]	remove format	[Ctrl] [Spacebar]

ACTIVITY 4.4

Formatting with the Shortcut Keys

1. Select and apply character formatting using the shortcut keys.

    select the words All Division Heads

    press **[CTRL] [I]** *to italicize the words*

    click somewhere in the text area to remove the highlighting

2. Remove the formatting.

    select the same words and press **[CTRL]** *[Spacebar]*

    You can remove a specific format style by repeating the command that applied it, or you can remove all format styles by selecting the text and pressing [Ctrl] [Spacebar].

On Your Own

Below you can see how the document TRAVEL.WPS should appear after you have applied character formatting.

1. Make TRAVEL.WPS the active document. Highlight the entire document and remove any character formatting by pressing [Ctrl] [Spacebar].

2. Apply character formatting as shown.

HINT: Use the Repeat Format command to repeat the last format. Select and apply bold in the usual way to *FROM:*, then select the word *TO:* and press [Shift] [F7] to apply the last format again.

DSR CORPORATION

MEMO

FROM: Walter Wings, Transportation Coordinator

TO: All Division Heads

DATE: July 23, 1994

SUBJECT: Travel Vouchers

(1) It has come to my attention that an increasing number of travel vouchers are being processed <u>**without**</u> the necessary verification of expenses.

(2) Beginning August 1, 1994, vouchers will **not** be processed unless accompanied by a motel or hotel receipt for <u>each</u> night's lodging.

(3) Receipts will also be required for *client* entertainment, taxis, and any unusual expenses.

(4) Receipts will not be required for meals while on travel, but employees are *expected to live **within the present guidelines.***

Walter Wings
Travel Coordinator

3. Print the document if you like.

4. Remove the formatting from paragraphs (1) and (2).

5. Close TRAVEL.WPS and do not save the changes.

Fonts

A font is a combination of characteristics that determine the appearance of a character of text. A font may have:

Character—A character design such as Arial, Bookman Old Style, or Times New Roman.

Style—A style such as Arial Normal, **Arial Bold**, *Arial Italic*, ***Arial Bold Italic.***

Size— In Windows you may choose a size between 4 and 127 points; 72 points vertically is one inch. For example:

_{6 points}   14 points   # 24 points

P i t c h On a typewriter, every character takes the same amount of horizontal space. Pica at 10 characters per inch (CPI) and Elite at 12 CPI are examples of fixed-pitch fonts. In Works, the Courier New font is similar, except it will serve as either Pica or Elite. Oddly, 12-point Courier New would correspond to Pica (10 CPI), and 10-point Courier New corresponds to Elite (12 CPI). Remember, pitch is the number of characters per inch, so the smaller type will have the larger CPI.

Other fonts uses proportionally spaced type. With these fonts, such as Times New Roman and Arial, a character is given only the space it needs to be displayed. Some comparative examples are shown below.

```
Courier New 12 point (like Pica)
```
Times New Roman 12 point

```
Courier New 10 point (like Elite)
```
Times New Roman 10 point

```
Courier New 12 point      MOM MOM        I'll I'll
```
Times New Roman 12 point   **MOM MOM**   I'll I'll

This means that, while Courier will have 70 characters on a line if the text area is 7 inches wide, the number of Times New Roman characters on a line will vary according to the text. It is also the reason why you should never use spaces to align text, since with a proportionally spaced font, the width of characters, including spaces, varies with the content. Later you will learn how to use Works tabs to align text.

Font and Size Boxes

The easiest way to apply a font is to select the text and then choose from the *Font* and *Size* list boxes in the Toolbar. If you want to start typing in a different font, choose the font and size before you begin. The current font and size at the insertion point are shown in the list boxes. If the name and size of a font don't appear, it's because your selection contains more than one font or size. Click the *Font* or *Size* boxes to show the lists. If the font size you want is not listed, type in the desire value.

ACTIVITY 4.5
Formatting with a Different Font

1. Open TRAVEL.WPS from the student diskette.

2. Apply a font to the document titles.

   select the words DSR CORPORATION *and* MEMO

   scroll up through the Font *list box and click Arial*

3. Apply a size to the titles.

   select the words DSR CORPORATION

   scroll through the Size *box and click the number 18*

   select the word MEMO

   scroll through the Size *box and click the number 14*

   click somewhere in the text area to remove highlighting

4. Leave the document open for the next activity.

Word Processor

Formatting with the Font and Style Command

Perhaps you have hidden the Toolbar. You may still change the character format of text from the menu. Choosing Format, Font and Style will display the *Font and Style* dialog box.

Not only does the *Font and Style* dialog box let you choose a font and size, but you may also add a style and even a color. Naturally, the color won't print on a black and white printer but it makes your on-screen document more striking. The dialog box also shows a sample of how the font will appear in the document. You may do one other important task with the dialog box. By clicking the Set Default button you will set the currently selected font and size as the defaults whenever you create a document.

ACTIVITY 4.6

Character Formatting from the Menu

1. Be sure TRAVEL.WPS is the active document.

2. Change the font for the title using the menu.

   select the title DSR CORPORATION

   choose Format, Font and Style

   from the Font and Style *dialog box choose Times New Roman, 24 point, bold*

   choose a color (dark colors look best)

   click OK

click somewhere in the text to remove the selection

5. Print if you like. Close the document without saving the changes.

Special Characters

In addition to the alphabetic and punctuation characters, a Windows font includes special characters such as •, ®, and §. These characters may be inserted by holding down the [Alt] key and typing a number on the numeric keypad. Here are some examples of symbols you can insert into text:

Alt code	Symbol	Alt Code	Symbol
0174	®	0167	§
0149	•	0187	»

You can find other codes and symbols by opening the Character Map utility program in the Windows 3.1 Program Manager.

Paragraph Formatting

Like character formatting, paragraph formatting is used to improve the appearance of your document and to organize or call attention to important sections of the text. You can easily set indents or line spacing or align paragraphs. As with character formatting, you will be using the Toolbar, shortcut keys, and the menu. With paragraph formatting you can:

- Indent right and left margins.

- Provide an exact first-line indent.

- Indent with the menu and the Ruler.

- Format a paragraph with a hanging indent where the first-line indent is to the left of the rest of the paragraph.

- Align paragraphs to the left, the right, or the center, or justify the paragraph.

- Add space before or after a paragraph.

- Change the spacing of lines in point-sized increments.

- Add bullets to a paragraph.

- Add a border around a paragraph.

- Ensure that a paragraph appears in its entirety on one page, or that two paragraphs remain together on a single page.

Word Processor

Indenting from the Menu

The Format, Paragraph command introduces a new type of dialog box. Rather than clutter a single dialog box with a multitude of choices, the box is divided by tabs into three sections. This enables you to work with one group of options at a time. One of the groups allows you to apply Quick Formats to your work using default settings. To view the additional options click the appropriate tab. Look at the sample shown in the dialog box to see how your choices will affect the appearance of the paragraph.

You can use the *Paragraph* dialog box to change paragraph indention, line spacing, alignment, and to tell Works how you want to treat paragraphs that occur near the end of a page. To format a single paragraph it is only necessary to have the insertion point somewhere inside the paragraph. To format multiple paragraphs, select the paragraphs first, then apply the format. If a value is highlighted in a dialog box, you can immediately type over the value without erasing it. Here are some things you can do with paragraph formatting:

Indents—An indent is space added from the margin to the left or right or at both sides of a paragraph. Type a number in the *Left*, *Right* or *1st Line Indent* box. The number you type will have the dimensions (inches, centimeters, points or picas) you set in the *Units* options box of the Tool, Options dialog box. For other units, type in, cm, pt, or pi following the number.

Alignment—Right or left alignment formats a paragraph with an even left or right edge. With justified alignment, both edges are even, while with center alignment, each line of a paragraph is centered with both edges ragged.

Spacing Between Lines—Click the Breaks and Spacing tab to go to that section of the dialog box. Type *Auto* into the Space Between Lines if you want Works to set the line spacing for you. Lines that might have a larger font or contain subscript and superscript characters are set automatically to the best spacing for that line. Auto spacing is approximately 120 percent of the font point size. A 10-point font will be given a 12-point spacing. Type in another number if you want a larger or smaller spacing. The default dimension is lines (li): typing *2* in the text box will give two lines of spacing (double space). You can use other dimensions as well. Be careful not to type 12 in the Spacing Between Lines box if you really mean 12 points.

Before Paragraphs—This provides space before each selected paragraph. Use Space Before Paragraph instead of adding a line between paragraphs. Use the same dimensions as Spacing Between Lines.

After Paragraphs—Extra space is put after the paragraph.

Don't break paragraph—If Works would normally break a paragraph at the end of a page, Don't Break Paragraph will force the entire paragraph to the next page.

Keep paragraph with next—A paragraph thus formatted will remain on the same page with the following paragraph. This would prevent the title of a table and the table itself from falling on different pages.

Quick Formats

To quickly apply the most commonly used paragraph formats, use the Quick Formats section of the dialog box. The default tab stops determine the values used for indents. Be sure to select the paragraphs before applying Quick Formats.

Normal—Normal format removes any quick formats already applied to selected paragraphs.

Bulleted—This format inserts a bullet in the margin on the first line of the paragraph. The remainder of the paragraph is indented one tab stop.

Hanging Indent—A hanging indent is the opposite of the first-line indent. The first line starts at the left margin and the rest of the paragraph is indented one tab stop.

Quotation—The quotation format justifies the text and indents it from both the right and left margins.

Apply Relative To—The indents are applied either relative to the left margin or the current indent of the first selected paragraph.

ACTIVITY 4.7

Indenting Paragraphs

1. Open the ACME.WPS document from the student diskette. Show the non-printing characters.

2. Indent the first three paragraphs.

   show the non-printing characters

   select the first three paragraphs (the Acme address and date)

   choose Format, Paragraph

   click the Indents and Alignment tab

   *type **3.25"** in the Left text box*

   click OK

3. Indent a paragraph from the right and left.

   move the insertion point to paragraph (6)

   choose Format, Paragraph

   *type **.75** in the Left text box, then press* TAB *to move to the Right text box*

   *type **.75** in the Right Indent text box*

   click OK or press ENTER

ACTIVITY 4.8

Create a Hanging Indent and Bulleted Paragraph

1. Select paragraphs (3) and (4) in the document ACME.WPS.

2. Format a hanging indent.

   choose Format, Paragraph and click the Indents and Alignment tab

   *type **.5** in the Left box*

   *type **-.5** in the 1st Line box*

   click OK

The paragraphs are indented .5 inches, but the first line of each paragraph is not. The first line has been moved back −.5 inches to the left of the remainder of the paragraph.

3. Add a bullet.

    move the insertion point to the left of the first character in paragraph (3), the left parenthesis

    hold down **ALT** *and type* **0164** *on the numeric keypad*

    press **TAB**

    add a bullet to paragraph (4) in the same manner

4. Save the document by another name.

    choose File, Save As

    type **MYACME** *in the* File Name *box and press* **ENTER**

Adding Space Before or After a Paragraph

It is best to add the exact space you want before or after a paragraph rather than to insert an extra line. Later, if you decide to change the spacing, just select the paragraphs and change the spacing value. In the next activity you will remove the extra lines added between paragraphs and replace them with the space you specify.

ACTIVITY 4.9

Adding Space Between Paragraphs

1. Remove the extra lines from MYACME.WPS.

    show the non-printing characters

    select the entire document

    choose Edit, Replace

    in the Find What *box type* **^p^p**

    in the Replace With *box type* **^p**

    click Replace All, then click Close

2. Add space after the selected paragraphs.

    select paragraphs (1) through (7)

    choose Format, Paragraph and click the Breaks and Spacing tab

    type **1.2** *in the* Space After Paragraph *box and click OK*

    click in the text area to remove the highlighting

3. Add space after the beginning paragraphs.

    select the paragraph January 24, 1993 *(near the top of the document)*

    add .6 lines after the paragraph

    select the paragraphs Bethesda, MD 22003 *and* Gentlemen:

    add .6 lines after the paragraphs

4. The spacing between the remaining paragraphs is too large. Change the paragraph spacing.

    select paragraphs (1) through (7) if they are not already selected

    choose Format, Paragraph

    type **.5** *in the* After Paragraphs *box and click OK*

    click in the text area to remove the highlighting

5. Add 1 inch of spacing after *Yours truly,*. Save your work.

Paragraph Alignment

You can align a paragraph either from the Format, Paragraph menu or by using the alignment icons on the Toolbar. The Left, Center, and Right alignment icons are to the right of the character formatting icons.

ACTIVITY 4.10

Aligning Paragraphs

1. Justify the main paragraphs.

    select paragraphs (1) through (7)

    choose Format, Paragraph and click the Indents and Alignment tab

    click the Justified option button

2. Center the closing.

    select the paragraphs from Yours truly, *to the end of the document*

    click the Center Alignment icon in the Toolbar

Line Spacing

You can make the line spacing in a paragraph single, double, or triple space, or any value you choose (within reason, of course).

ACTIVITY 4.11
Changing Line Spacing

1. Change the line spacing within a paragraph.

    move the insertion point somewhere in paragraph (6)

    choose Format, Paragraph and click the Breaks and Spacing tab

    replace the word Auto *by typing* **1.5** *in the* Between Lines *text box*

    click OK

    make the text in the paragraph bold

2. Save your work (you should be using the document MYACME.WPS), but do not close the document.

Adding a Border Around a Paragraph

You can add a border around a paragraph or selected paragraphs with the Format, Border command.

*   Choose from one of three line style options and several colors.

*   Click the Outline check box if you want the border to surround the selected paragraphs.

*   Click the Top, Bottom, Left, and/or Right check boxes if you want a partial border.

*   To remove a border, select the paragraph or paragraphs, then clear the checks from all boxes in the *Border* dialog box.

Word Processor

ACTIVITY 4.12

Adding a Border to a Paragraph

1.   Create a border.

   move the insertion point to paragraph (6)

   choose Format, Border

   mark the Outline check box

   mark the Double line style option

   pick a color if you wish

   click OK to add the border

2.   Remove the border.

   with the insertion point in paragraph (6), choose Format, Border

   remove all check marks from the Border *dialog box*

   click OK to remove the border

3.   Clean up and save the document.

   remove the numbers and their parentheses at the beginning of the paragraphs

   save the document

4.   Print if you wish. Close the document.

Quick Formats

You can also add one of several default formats to a paragraph with Quick Formats. Any of these formats may be duplicated from the Format, Paragraph menu.

elf

ACTIVITY 4.13

Quick Paragraph Formatting

1. Open the document ACME.WPS.

2. Try a Quick Format.

    select paragraph (6)

    choose Format, Paragraph and click the Quick Formats tab

    mark the Quotation and Left Margin options

    click OK

3. Return to normal paragraph formatting.

    with paragraph (6) still selected choose Format, Paragraph

    mark the Normal option

    click OK

4. Close ACME.WPS without saving changes.

The Paragraph Format Shortcut Keys

You can also use shortcut keys to align paragraphs, change line spacing, and open a space before a paragraph. The paragraph formatting shortcut keys:

Alignment

center	[Ctrl] [E]	justify	[Ctrl] [J]
left	[Ctrl] [L]	right	[Ctrl] [R]

Indents

indent	[Ctrl] [N]	remove indent	[Ctrl] [M]

Spacing

single	[Ctrl] [1]
double	[Ctrl] [2]
space before paragraph	[Ctrl] [O]

Remove paragraph formatting

remove	[Ctrl] [Q]

Word Processor

Page Setup and Document Formatting

Document formatting involves setting margins, paper size, and page numbers. The margins are the white space that forms the perimeter of each page. Paragraph indents are measured from the inside edge of the margins. For example, a 1" left margin and a 0.5" left indent would show text starting 1.5" from the left edge of the paper. Page setup and document formatting are found in the File, Page Setup dialog box. You can:

- Set the document margins.

- Determine where headers and footers, including page numbers, will appear at the top or bottom of each page. Headers and footers are text that appear on each page.

- Choose a different size paper or page orientation.

ACTIVITY 4.14

Changing the Document Margins

1. Open ACME.WPS.

2. Change the top and bottom margins.

   choose File, Page Setup and click the Margins tab

   type **1** *in the* Top Margin *text box*

   type **1** *in the* Bottom Margin *text box*

   click OK

3. Close the document and do not save the changes.

On Your Own

In this On Your Own you will again go through the steps to format and print the ACME.WPS document, but this time with only a specification to go by.

1. Open ACME.WPS. Save the document by the name ACMEOYO.

2. Format the top three paragraphs (the address of Acme Corporation) with a left indent of 3.25". Format the date to have 0.6 lines after it.

3. Remove extra lines between paragraphs. Save your work.

4. Format the paragraphs *January 24, 1993*, *Bethesda, MD 22003*, and *Gentlemen:* to have 0.6 lines after them.

5. Format paragraphs (1) through (7) to have 0.5 lines after them.

6. Format paragraphs (3) and (4) to have hanging indents of 0.5". Add a bullet to each paragraph.

   or

   Use the Quick Formats to format a Bulleted paragraph. Save your work.

7. Format paragraph (6) to have a .75" left indent and a .75" right indent.

   or

   Use the Quick Formats to apply the Quotations format to the paragraph.

8. Format paragraphs (1) through (7) to be justified.

9. Add 1" of space after the paragraph *Yours truly,*.

10. Center the closing from *Yours truly,* to the end of the document.

11. Remove the paragraph numbers and parentheses. Save and print the document. Compare the two versions.

12. Make the top margin 1.2" and the bottom margin 1". Format the entire document in Times New Roman, 12 point.

13. Choose File, Print Preview and view the document as it would print. Make any changes you think necessary.

14. Save, print, and close the document.

Tabs and the Ruler

When the Ruler is displayed, it shows the tabs and indents for the paragraph containing the insertion point. You can use the Ruler to set tabs and indents or to move them once they have been set. If the Ruler does not appear at the top of your document, choose View, Ruler.

Indents—If a paragraph has a 0" left and 0" first-line indent this is indicated by a split arrowhead at the left end of the Ruler (left margin). The top half of the arrowhead represents the first-line indent and the bottom half, the left indent. In the figure above, the paragraph has a 0" left indent and 0.5" first-line indent. The right indent mark, show in the Ruler at 4.5", is a solid arrowhead pointing left.

- **Dragging the Left Indent.** When you drag the left indent (bottom half of the arrowhead), the top half (first-line indent) moves with it. To move the left indent independently, hold the [Shift] key down as you drag it.

- **Dragging the First-Line Indent.** The first-line indent can be dragged independent of the left indent. If you want to drag them together, drag the left indent marker.

- **Dragging the Right Indent.** The right indent is a solid arrowhead and can be dragged with the mouse.

Tabs—Works provides four types of tabs—right, left, center, and decimal. When you begin a document, default tabs show as inverted T's set at 0.5" intervals. Default tabs are left-aligned.

- If you press [Tab] to go to a left-aligned tab, text will be inserted to the right of the tab as you type.

- If you press [Tab] to go to a right-aligned tab, text will be inserted to the left of the tab as you type.

- If you press [Tab] to go to a center-aligned tab, text will be inserted both to the left and right to center about the tab.

- If you press [Tab] to go to a decimal-aligned tab, the number will be inserted so the decimal point will be at the tab position.

- Once a tab has been set, you may drag it to a new position.

- Tabs apply only to the paragraphs that were selected when the tabs were set.

In the Ruler shown above, a left tab is shown at 1", a center tab at 1.5", a right tab at 2", a decimal tab at 2.5" and default tabs at 3", 3.5", and 4".

Setting Tabs

You may set tab positions using the Format, Tabs menu or by clicking on the Ruler. Always remember to first select the paragraph or paragraphs where the tabs are to take effect.

You add a tab by choosing Format, Tabs and typing in a value in the *Position* box and clicking an alignment in the *Alignment* option box. If you would like a leader, a series of dots or other characters that lead back to the previous tab, select a Leader option, then click OK. To delete a tab, first select the tab and then choose Delete from the *Tabs* dialog box, or drag the tab down from the Ruler until it disappears.

ACTIVITY 4.15

Building a Simple Table Using the Menu

1. Create a word processor document.

    choose File, Create New File and click Word Processor

    choose View, Ruler if the Ruler doesn't appear at the top of the new document

2. Add space at the top of the document.

    press  *4 times to insert 4 blank lines*

3. Set tabs.

    move the insertion point before the second paragraph mark

    choose Format, Tabs

    in the Position *box type* **1.5**

    click Left in the Alignment *box, then click the Insert button to set the first tab*

    in the Position *box type* **4**

    click Decimal in the Alignment *box and 1 in the* Leader *box*

    click the Insert button to set the second tab

    click OK to set the tabs

4. Type in the table to look like the one below.

    press TAB *then type* **Rent**

    press TAB *then type* **$460.00**

    press ENTER

    press TAB *then type* **Car expenses**

    press 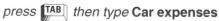 TAB *then type* **$45.00** *press* ENTER

press TAB *then type* **Amusements**

press TAB *then type* **$29.45**

press ENTER

```
Rent............................................... $460.00
Car expenses................................ $45.00
Amusements .................................. $29.45
```

5. Move the decimal tab.

    select the three paragraphs in the table

    drag the decimal tab to 5 inches on the Ruler

6. Close the document without saving the changes.

More about Tabs and Tables

In the next activity you will format an existing table to look like the one below. There is an easy way to set tabs using the Ruler. If you click once on the Ruler it will set a left-aligned tab at the point where you click. If you double-click on the Ruler it will take you to the *Tabs* dialog box where you can set a different alignment or add a leader to the tab.

ACTIVITY 4.16

Formatting a Table with Tabs

1. Open the document INSTABS.WPS from the student diskette and prepare to format the table.

    show the non-printing characters

    Notice that the tabs have already been typed into the table at the bottom of the memo but their positions have not been set.

2. Set a right-aligned tab.

    select the body of the table (5 lines), but not the heading

    double-click at 1.25" on the Ruler

Did you notice that the 1.25" was already entered into the *Position* text box?

click the right alignment button to set a right-aligned tab

click OK

3. Set a center-aligned tab.

double-click at 1.75" on the Ruler

click the Center option button in the Alignment *box*

click OK

4. Set three more tabs in a similar fashion.

set a left-aligned tab at 2.25" (click once for a left-aligned tab)

set a decimal-aligned tab at 3.75"

set a center-aligned tab at 4.25"

The center-aligned tab is too close. It needs to be reset.

drag the center-aligned tab from 4.25" to 4.75"

5. Set tabs for the table header.

select the header only

set a center tab above the center of each table column except the To column

drag the tabs to adjust the header for the best appearance

hide the non-printing characters

6. Print the memo if you wish. Close the file but do not save the changes.

ORIGIN	DESTINATION		FARE	CLASS
Washington	To	Denver	$ 86.53	First class
Denver	To	Seattle	$ 61.23	Tourist
Seattle	To	Hawaii	$225.98	First class
Hawaii	To	Washington	$372.34	Economy
	Total Fare		$746.08	

ACTIVITY 4.17

Setting Indents with the Ruler

1. Open the file ACME.WPS from the student diskette.

2. Create a hanging indent.

   select paragraphs (3) and (4)

   in the Ruler, drag the left indent marker (bottom half of the arrowhead) to .5"

   The first-line indent moves with the indent marker.

   drag the first-line indent marker back to 0"

3. Indent a paragraph from both margins.

   move the insertion point to paragraph (6)

   drag the left indent marker to .75" and the right indent marker to 4.75"

4. Close the document and do not save the changes.

On Your Own

1. Type in the table below using tab alignments of right, center, left, decimal, and center, respectively, for the five columns. Try to center the table on the page and choose tab positions that make it the most attractive. Do you find it easier to type the table first and then position the tabs, or do the tabs first and then type the text?

ORIGIN	DESTINATION		FARE	CLASS
Washington	To	Denver	$ 86.53	First class
Denver	To	Seattle	$ 61.23	Tourist
Seattle	To	Hawaii	$225.98	First class
Hawaii	To	Washington	$372.34	Economy
	Total Fare		$746.08	

Quick Check

1. What are three ways to apply character formatting?

2. How do you remove character style formatting?

3. How can you add a bullet character to a paragraph?

4. What are two ways to indent a paragraph?

5. Name the four types of tabs and explain how each formats text.

6. What command is used to change margins?

7. What is a font?

8. How do you remove paragraph formatting?

9. How can you use the Replace command to learn how many paragraphs are in a document?

10. How would you format the formula for water, H_2O, to subscript the 2 and format it in a smaller point size?

11. What is the difference between pitch (characters per inch) and points?

Proofing and Refining

5

Overview

After creating, editing, and formatting your document, you may want to add a header or footer, page numbers, and perhaps footnotes. You will also want to make a final check for errors and make sure that pages end where you expect them to before you save and print for the final time. Works' proofing features can quickly find and supply corrections for many common errors. In this chapter you'll learn how to use the proofing tools plus some special Works features.

Objectives

- Add headers and footers with page numbers

- Add footnotes

- Use the spelling checker and thesaurus

- Insert special placeholder characters that stand for dates and times

- Paginate your documents

- Learn how to use your printer with Works

Headers and Footers

Headers and footers are a way of making the same information appear at the top and bottom of each page. Headers and footers may contain text, page numbers, dates, or even graphics. You can create a simple header or footer with the Edit, Headers & Footers command or more complex paragraphs with the word processor.

- In most documents the first page doesn't have a header or footer, so Works permits you to start with the second page if you choose.

- Headers and footers are printed in the top and bottom margins of the page. To control their position, choose File, Page Setup and click the Margins tab. Type a value in the *Header Margin* and *Footer Margin* text boxes.

- Headers and footers do not normally appear on screen but can be viewed in Page Preview.

Print Preview

A great advantage of Windows programs is their portrayal on screen of the way your work will be printed. Even so, certain items that are on every page or that might be confusing, are sometimes omitted from your normal view of a document. To see how the final page will look, use the Print Preview command.

- You can view your entire page in reduced view or you can zoom in to see detail.

- You cannot edit in Print Preview.

ACTIVITY 5.1

Adding a Simple Header and Footer

1. Open the document TRUST.WPS from the student diskette.

2. Create a header and footer.

   choose View, Headers and Footers

   be sure the Use Header and Footer Paragraphs check box is not marked

   in the Header *box type* **Family Trust**

   in the Footer *box type* **DSR Corp**.

   mark the No Header on 1st Page and No Footer on 1st Page check boxes

   click OK

3. View the header and footer.

   click the Print Preview icon on the Toolbar (the magnifying glass)

   The first page of the document appears as it would print.

   click the Next button to go to the next page and note the header and footer

   click the Zoom In button to get an enlarged view of the page

   As you move the mouse pointer into the document, it becomes a magnifying glass. You can also click in the document to zoom at the point where you click. Works gives you two levels of zoom.

use the scroll bars to view the header and footer

click the Zoom Out button to return to page view

use the Next and Previous buttons to browse the rest of the document

4. Leave the document on screen for the next activity.

More Complex Headers and Footers

You can type more complex headers and footers as special paragraphs added to the top of your document by marking the Use header and footer paragraphs check box in the *Headers & Footers* dialog box.

*   When you use header and footer paragraphs, the letters H and F appear at the top of the document. Each letter represents a paragraph you may use for a header or footer by typing the text after the letter. Each paragraph comes with a center-aligned tab at the center of the page and a right-aligned tab at the right margin of the page. You may change these if you wish.

*   In the F paragraph Works has positioned the words *Page - *page** in the center of the footer. The **page** is a placeholder for the actual page number that will appear in its place in Print Preview and when you print. On page 3 the footer would appear as *Page - 3*. If you do not want the page number, erase the placeholder.

*   You can add other special characters like dates or times to the header or footer paragraphs by means of the Insert, Special Character command. These characters can also be inserted anywhere in your text.

*   You can also format the text in the header and footer using the usual formatting techniques.

ACTIVITY 5.2
Using Header and Footer Paragraphs

1. Delete the old header and footer from TRUST.WPS.

    choose View, Headers and Footers

    select and delete the text from the Header *and* Footer *text boxes*

Word Processor

2. Prepare for header and footer paragraphs.

    click the Use Header and Footer Paragraphs check box

    click OK, then press `CTRL` `HOME` *to go to the top of the document*

    Notice the H and F at the top of the document in the left margin.

3. Add a header.

    move the insertion point to the left end of the line marked H *at the top of the document*

    press `TAB` *to move to the center-aligned tab at the center of the header*

    type **DSR Corporation**

    press `ENTER` *to start a new header paragraph*

    press `TAB` *and type* **Law at your Service**

4. Add a footer.

    move the insertion point to the left end of the line marked F *at the top of the document*

    type **Family Trust**

5. Insert a special date character.

    press the `END` *key to skip past* Page - *page**

    press `TAB` *to move to the right-aligned tab*

    choose Insert, Special Character

    mark the Print Long Date option and click OK

6. View the header and footer with Print Preview.

7. Close the document without saving the changes.

Footnotes

A footnote can be used to refer to citations or make comments outside the body of the text. Each footnote consists of a reference number or mark in the text and the text or comment at the end of the page. If you choose number footnotes, they are consecutively numbered.

- To create a footnote, move the insertion point to where the reference number is to appear, then choose Insert, Footnote. If you want to use reference numbers, mark that option. If you want to use marks, click that option and type in the character you want to use in the *Mark* box. When you click OK, a footnote pane will appear at the bottom of the screen. Type in the text for your footnote.

- Choose View, Footnotes to show or hide the Footnote pane.

- If you want to edit the footnote text, show the Footnote pane and click in the pane or press [F6] to move there. Edit the text.

- To delete a footnote, select and delete the reference number or mark.

- To move a footnote reference, cut and paste it to a new location.

- To select where footnotes are to appear choose File, Page Setup and click the Other Options tab. Mark the Print footnotes at end of document check box if you do not want footnotes at the bottom of the page.

ACTIVITY 5.3
Adding Footnotes

1. Open the document MED.WPS from the student diskette.

2. Select a place for the footnotes.

   choose File, Page Setup and click the Other Options tab

   clear the Print footnotes at end of document check box

3. Insert a numbered footnote.

   move to paragraph 2, to the end of the word terminated *on line 4*

   choose Insert, Footnote

   mark the Numbered option in the Footnote *dialog box and click OK*

   in the Footnote pane, type **Do we really terminate our employees, or do we discharge them?**

choose View, Footnotes to remove the check mark from the command and close the Footnote pane

select the reference number 1 and change the character format to 8 point

4. Insert another footnote.

    move to paragraph 4, to the end of the first sentence

    insert a footnote by typing **Bills shall be submitted to the Payroll Dept**.

    change the character format of the reference number to 8 point

5. View the footnotes.

    click the Print Preview icon to view the page and footnotes

6. Delete the second footnote.

    select footnote reference 2

    choose Edit, Cut to remove the reference and associated text

7. Close the document and do not save the changes.

Checking Spelling

The Works spelling checker uses a standard dictionary to check for spelling errors. Not every word is in the dictionary, nor would you want that to be the case, because you want Works to find typographical errors as well as misspellings. If the archaic word *thee* was in Works' dictionary, then the word *thee* that appeared as a typo for *the* in your text would not be considered an error.

In addition, many technical words are not included. You may add technical words, names, and other expressions to a custom dictionary so Works won't consider them misspellings. Click the Add button in the *Spelling* dialog box. You may begin a spelling check from the Toolbar, or by clicking the icon that shows a check mark with the letters ABC over it, or by using the Tools, Spelling command.

The Tools, Spelling dialog box prompts you for decisions as you spell check a document. Word first finds a word that is not in the dictionary, then displays it in the *Spelling* dialog box.

Spelling

Not in Dictionary: reciept

Change To: receipt

Suggestions:
- receipt
- recouped

Ignore   Ignore All
Change   Change All
Add   Cancel
Suggest   Help

☐ Skip capitalized words
☒ Always Suggest

If the word is incorrectly spelled, you have several choices:

- In the *Change To* box, you can type in a correction if you know the correct spelling.

- If you're not sure how to spell the word, you may choose a word from the *Suggestions* list by clicking the Suggest button or if the Always Suggest check box is marked.

- When the correction is selected, choose Change if you want just that word changed, or choose Change All if you want the word changed throughout the document.

If the word is correctly spelled, but not in the dictionary, you can:

- Add the word to the custom dictionary by clicking the Add button.

  or

- You may ignore the word. If you ignore it, choose Ignore for just that single word, or choose Ignore All to ignore the word throughout the document.

Other facts about the Spell Checker that you may find helpful:

- Like Find and other proofing tools, the spelling check begins at the insertion point and proceeds to the end of the document.

- You may check just a portion of your text by selecting it first.

- To check a single word, double-click the word and click the Spell icon.

Word Processor

ACTIVITY 5.4

Checking the Spelling of a Document

1. Open the document CHECK.WPS from the student diskette.

2. Start the spelling check.

    click the Spell icon on the Toolbar

    make the corrections shown in the table on the next page

    choose OK when the spelling check is complete

3. Leave the document open for the next activity.

    CORRECTIONS

From	To
WITNESSETH	spelled correctly, Ignore or Ignore All
transfered	transferred
parte	part
reciept	receipt
acnowledges	acknowledges
acordance	accordance
ayone	anyone
policys	policies
uncollectable	uncollectible
seperate	separate
Trusteee	Trustee
ments	*installments (see note)
quarterannuallly	quarter annually
b.The	b. The
to to	to (choosing Change will delete the duplicated word)
fulfiling	fulfilling

NOTE: The word *installments* was typed with an extra space between *install* and *ments*. Correcting only the *ments* will leave an extra *install* in the text. During the spelling check, place an asterisk by the corrected word in the *Change To* box. When you have finished the spelling check, use the Edit, Find command to search for the asterisk. Remove the extra *install* and the asterisk.

Using the Thesaurus

The thesaurus provides a way of finding words with similar meanings that might help make your writing more precise.

```
┌──────────────────────── Thesaurus ────────────────────────┐
│ Synonyms for: quickly                            ┌─────────┐│
│ Meanings:              Synonyms:                  │ Change  ││
│ ┌─────────────┐  ┌─────────────────┐             ├─────────┤│
│ │fast (a)     │  │instantly        │             │ Suggest ││
│ │immediately (a)│ │instantaneously │             ├─────────┤│
│ │             │  │directly         │             │ Cancel  ││
│ │             │  │forthwith        │             ├─────────┤│
│ │             │  │promptly         │             │  Help   ││
│ │             │  │soon             │             └─────────┘│
│ └─────────────┘  └─────────────────┘                       │
└────────────────────────────────────────────────────────────┘
```

To find a synonym for a word:

- Move the insertion point into the word or into the space immediately following it.
- Choose Tools, Thesaurus.
- Because a word may have more than one meaning, choose the meaning you want from the *Meanings* box. The words are followed by a letter indicating their part of speech, (a) adjective, (v) verb, or (n) noun.
- When you have chosen a meaning, the synonyms for the word appear in the *Synonyms* list box. Select the one that best fits the context and click the Change button.
- To find a synonym of a synonym, select the synonym and click the Suggest button.

ACTIVITY 5.5

Choosing a Synonym

1. Make CHECK.WPS the active document.
2. Select a word and find a synonym.

   use Edit, Find to locate the word quickly

   place the insertion point within the word

   choose Tools, Thesaurus

Word Processor

in the Meanings *box, choose* immediately

choose promptly *in the* Synonyms *box*

click the Change button

3. Find a better word for *complete* in paragraph 1. Leave the document open for the next activity.

Hyphenation

Hyphenation is used to produce a less ragged right margin. Works will hyphenate an entire document or show you where to hyphenate a single word.

```
┌────────────────────────────────────────────────────┐
│ ─                    Hyphenation                     │
├────────────────────────────────────────────────────┤
│                                                      │
│  Hyphenate At:   │pre-mi-um│s              │          │
│                                                      │
│  ☒ Hyphenate CAPS              Hot Zone: │0.25″│     │
│  ☐ Confirm            ┌───────┐ ┌──────┐ ┌────────┐ │
│                       │  Yes  │ │  No  │ │ Cancel │ │
│                       └───────┘ └──────┘ └────────┘ │
└────────────────────────────────────────────────────┘
```

*   When non-printing characters are hidden, hyphens only appear when the word breaks at the end of a line.

*   Works may give you more than one choice for the position of a hyphen. Click the hyphen you want to break the word.

*   The Hot Zone gives the width of the ragged margin within which Works will hyphenate. A small Hot Zone provides a less ragged margin and more hyphens.

ACTIVITY 5.6

Hyphenating a Word

1. Make CHECK.WPS the active document and turn on the non-printing characters.

    choose View, All Characters

2. Hyphenate a word.

    select the word acknowledges *near the end of line 4 in paragraph 1*

    choose Tools, Hyphenation

    click the second hyphen in the Hyphenate At *box*

click Yes

The hyphen appears in the word.

choose View, All Characters to hide the non-printing characters

The hyphen is hidden.

3.   Delete the hyphen.

choose View, All Characters to show the non-printing characters

select and delete the hyphen

4.   Close the document without saving the changes.

Special Characters

You have already used some of the special characters that Works provides for page numbers and dates. Four other special characters are of interest for editing text. To insert a special character, move the insertion point to where it is to appear. Then choose the character from the Insert, Special Character options box or use the shortcut key if one is available.

End-of-Line Mark—Starts a new line without ending a paragraph. This mark is frequently used in tables at the end of each line instead of pressing [Enter], making the entire table a single paragraph. The shortcut key for the end-of-line mark is [Shift] [Enter].

Optional Hyphen—If non-printing characters are hidden, an optional hyphen shows only when a word breaks at the end of a line. You must have the non-printing characters showing in order to delete an optional hyphen. The shortcut key is [Ctrl] [Hyphen].

Non-Breaking Hyphen—You use a non-breaking hyphen to override word wrap in order to keep hyphenated words on the same line. The shortcut key is [Ctrl] [Shift] [Hyphen].

Non-Breaking Space—Like the non-breaking hyphen, a non-breaking space overrides word wrap to keep words with spaces between them on the same line. The shortcut key is [Ctrl] [Shift] [Spacebar].

The rest of the special characters insert the document filename or a page, date, or time. To find a brief description of each special character, choose Insert, Special Character, then click each option box and read the explanation in the dialog box.

Word Processor

Pagination

Pagination affects where pages begin in a document. Based on margins, fonts, paper size, the number of lines typed, and other formatting considerations, Works will decide where each page in a multi-page document should end. At each page end, Works inserts automatic, or soft, page breaks. If you add text, change margins, or do anything else that affects the length of text on a page, Works recalculates the position of the soft page break on that and each subsequent page. A soft page break is shown by a » character in the left margin at the beginning of the page.

You may choose where a page ends by inserting a hard page break in the text. Works will recalculate the position of the soft page breaks on following pages. While Works may move a soft page break due to editing, it will not change the location of a hard page break. A hard page break is shown by a dotted line across the page.

Works always repaginates your document while printing. For this reason, you should preview a document as the last step before printing to be sure that page breaks will occur where you want. Before you print, spell check the document. On rare occasions the spelling of a word might change the location of a page break. While it is relatively simple to manage page breaks in a short document, pagination of a longer document requires an understanding of how Works chooses the location of each page break. Here are some Works features that can help with pagination:

- The File, Print Preview command repaginates before displaying.

- Works repaginates your documents automatically in the intervals when you are not typing or editing.

- You can use the Format, Indents & Spacing dialog box to prevent a page break from occurring within a paragraph.

- You can also use the Format, Paragraph dialog box to keep consecutive paragraphs on the same page. Click the Breaks and Spacing tab. Marking the Keep paragraph with next check box will ensure that the selected paragraph is kept on the same page as the following paragraph. Marking the Don't break paragraph check box will keep the entire selected paragraph on the same page.

- You can use the Tools, Paginate Now command to have Works repaginate the document.

- Page Setup and Margins also influence the location of page breaks.

elf

Activity 5.7

Keeping Paragraphs and Lines Together

1. Open TRUST.WPS from the student diskette.

2. Format paragraphs to stay together.

    go to the top of page 2

    note the position of the page break (»)

    The heading for the clause will appear at the bottom of page 1 and the clause itself will appear on page 2.

    select the clause heading (1) Income to Settlors

    choose Format, Paragraph and click the Breaks and Spacing tab

    mark the Keep paragraph with next check box

    click OK

3. Allow Works to repaginate the document and watch the page break change.

    choose Tools, Paginate Now

4. Close the document and do not save the changes.

Hard Page Breaks

Hard page breaks may be added by moving the insertion point to the location in the document where the break is to occur and then choosing Insert, Page Break. You may also insert a hard page break by pressing [Ctrl] [Enter]. A hard page break can make a page shorter but never longer. To delete a hard page break, move the insertion point into the line containing the break and press [Delete]. You can't delete a soft page break.

Activity 5.8

Adding and Deleting Hard Page Breaks

1. Make TRUST.WPS the active document.

2. Add a hard page break.

    scroll down in the document to page 2

Word Processor

move the insertion point before the left parenthesis in (1)

press **CTRL** **ENTER** *to insert a hard page break*

Note that the » indicating the top of the page moves when Works repaginates the document.

3. Scroll through the document placing hard page breaks at appropriate locations.

    clause 9 on page 7 would be such a location

4. Delete a hard page break.

    move the insertion point into the last hard page break

    press **DEL** *to remove the break*

Reviewing Page Breaks in a Finished Document

After you have completed a document it is a good idea to review the page breaks before you print. After you have moved text around and added material in one place and deleted it another, you may find places where hard page breaks appear too close together, creating short pages.

On Your Own

1. Open the document TRUST.WPS.

2. Add a header and footer paragraph.

    H – *your name* Family Trust
    F – DSR Corporation   page #   print long date

    Center the header. Use the three tabs provided for the three parts to the footer.

3. Add hard page breaks as appropriate throughout.

4. Use Print Preview to look at the document.

Counting Words

You can count the words in a selection or the entire document with the Tools, Word Count command.

ACTIVITY 5.9

Counting the Words in a Document

1. Make TRUST.WPS the active document.

2. Count the words in the document.

    choose Tools, Word Count

3. Count the words in a selection.

    select a paragraph

    choose Tools, Word Count

4. Close the document and do not save the changes.

Preparing to Print

In the previous chapters, if you wanted to print a document, you simply clicked the Print icon. For more control over the printing process you will need to be concerned with the default values used for both the printer and the document. These are the values in effect when you choose the Print icon and the ones you would normally want to use. However, you may need to change the defaults to get the printed results you want. Here are the steps:

*   Choose File, Printer Setup to change the configuration for your printer. Works makes use of the Windows printer setup program to permit you to change these defaults. The *Printer Setup* dialog box shows the active printer in the *Printer* list box.

*   To make changes to your printer setup, click Setup in the *Printer Setup* dialog box. Setup permits you to change the paper size and orientation so that you can use larger paper or print in the Landscape (sideways) position. If you choose a different orientation or paper you must also change the paper size with the File, Page Setup command. The orientation and paper size must match. Portrait works with 8.5" by 11" paper. Landscape works with 11" by 8.5" paper.

Print Setup

For more information about printers read the printer section in the Windows 3.1 manual and the instructions that came with your printer. If you are only interested in a brief summary, read the information below.

Before you can use a printer with Windows you must install, configure, and set it up. The installation and configuration occurred during the installation of Windows 3.1.

Word Processor

Installation—When you install a printer you tell Windows 3.1 which file containing information about your printer (called a printer driver) should be used.

Configuration—Configuring a printer means connecting your printer driver to the proper computer port or connector. This ensures that information goes to the same connector to which the printer is attached.

Setup—Setting up a printer means selecting options for your particular use of the printer, for example, choosing 8.5" by 11" or 8.5" by 14" paper, printing in portrait or landscape orientation, or selecting letter quality or draft mode.

ACTIVITY 5.10

Printing a Landscape Page

1. Open the document POSTER.WPS from the student diskette.

2. Print the poster (or click the Print Preview icon).

   click the Print icon

3. Change the paper size for landscape printing.

   choose File, Page Setup and click the Source, Size, and Orientation tab

   click the Landscape option button

   click OK

   The paper is now set for the correct size and orientation.

4. Change the printer setup to landscape.

   choose File, Printer Setup and press the Setup button in the dialog box

   click the Landscape button, then OK twice to return to your document

   The printer is now set to agree with the paper size and orientation.

5. Print the poster (or click the Print Preview icon).

6. Change the paper size and printer setup back to their original values.

7. Close the document and do not save the changes.

Case Study

By now, you have gone through all the steps necessary for creating, editing, formatting, proofing, and printing a polished final document. Put all that you have learned to work in this case study. The next page shows a final report page. The document FINRPT.WPS on your student diskette contains the basic text. To produce the finished document, these are the steps:

1. Open FINRPT.WPS from the student diskette. Show the non-printing characters.

2. Make the top and bottom margins 0.8".

3. Select the entire document and make the font Times New Roman, 11 pt.

4. Make the title, *ACME UNIFORM SERVICE*, Arial 13 point, bold. Make the next two lines Arial. Center the top four paragraphs.

5. Bold and underline other text as shown in the example.

6. Table 1 tabs:

    table tabs—1. left tab at 1.75", 2. decimal tab at 4.0"
    heading tabs set for best appearance

7. Table 2 tabs:

    table tabs—1. left at 0.5", 2. left at 1.5", 3. left at 3.25", 4. decimal at 5"
    heading tabs set for best appearance

8. Center the table headings.

9. Space before or after paragraphs:

    first line of title block—0 lines
    third line of title block— 0.8 lines after
    final paragraph before closing block (Submitted by:)—1.5 lines after
    body paragraphs—0.3 lines after
    table headings—0.7 lines before, 0.3 lines after
    tables—none

10. Indents:

    first paragraph—none
    closing block—none
    other paragraphs, except subheadings—0.2"

11. After formatting the document, replace the word *second* with *third* throughout.

12. Check your spelling.

13. Print and close the original document without saving the changes.

Word Processor

ACME UNIFORM SERVICE
Tri-State Sales Report
Third Quarter, 1992

Report Summary

This report is intended to summarize the Tri-State sales for the third quarter of 1992. It consists of tables showing the Second Quarter Sales for 1992, and the orders by key accounts in that quarter.

Sales figures

Table 1 lists the sales figures for the six sub-regions within the Acme Uniform Service sales and service area and compares them with the figures for 1991. As the table shows, sales have improved moderately within all but the Mideast sub-region.

Table 1. **Third Quarter Sub-Regional Sales and Service**

Sub-Region	Revenues
Northeast	351,200
Southeast	429,650
Midwest	183,600
Mideast	236,750
Northwest	311,600
Southwest	410,330
Total	1,923,130

Midwest Sub-region

The Midwest sub-region shows the largest sales increase with an 8.1% change compared with last year. Unfortunately, the Midwest and Northeast sub-regions were the only ones to exceed the inflation rate for the 12 month period ending 30 September. While we realize that economic conditions in general have not been good, still, every sub-region should be doing better. Let's Clean Up!

Orders

Orders for the year are up over 1991. Table 2 gives the size of the orders placed by our key accounts throughout the region during the second quarter.

Table 2. **Orders Placed by Key Accounts**

Sub-Region	Account	Sales Rep.	Order
Northeast	Grit & Grime Inc.	P. Sideswipe	18,000
Southeast	Janco	A. Walters	12,000
Midwest	Mop 'em Up	R. Limpear	14,500
	Scrub 'em Down	W. Wilson	11,000
Mideast	Triple C	B. Edge	17,200
Northwest	CleanCo	E. Bright	40,500
Southwest	Rinse Away	W. Wipewell, Jr.	26,000

Submitted by:

Sandra A. Williams
Regional Sales Manager
November 23, 1992

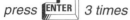
ACTIVITY 5.11

Just for Fun

1. Create a word processor document.

2. Type in text.

    press ⏎ENTER *3 times*

    type **Here is a note just for you!**

    format the note as Arial, 18 point

    center the text by pressing the shortcut key CTRL E

    press ⏎ENTER *and change the character format to Arial 12 point*

    press ⏎ENTER *4 more times*

3. Add a special note.

    choose Insert, Note-It

    click an icon of your choice in the Choose a Picture *box*

    type **MY NOTE TO YOU** *to replace the text in the* Type Your Caption Here *box below the* Choose a Picture *box*

    in the Type Your Note Here *box type:*

    > **Are you going to the picnic?**
    > **If you are, I'll pick you up at 12:45.**
    > **Hope you can go!**

    click the Small Text option, then click OK

4. Deliver your note.

    double-click the picture in your document

5. Close the document and do not save the changes.

Word Processor

Quick Check

1. How would you add page numbers to a document?

2. How would you print only pages 5, 6, and 7 of a document?

3. What automatic information can be included in a header or footer?

4. What are the steps in adding a footnote? moving a footnote?

5. What is the last step you should take before printing a document?

6. To avoid the appearance of your company name as an error every time you use the spelling checker, what should you do?

7. What does a thesaurus do?

8. What are the steps in printing a landscape document?

Applets, Templates, and Wizards

6

Overview

Works 3.0 for Windows consists of four separate but integrated programs, plus accessory techniques that make the four more versatile and easier to use.

Applets are small applications that are a part of the Works package. WordArt is an applet designed to give your word processor documents and database forms a special look by providing fancy fonts and text designs. Microsoft Draw is a basic drawing program you can use to create and modify illustrations that you can place in your documents.

Templates are patterns for documents, spreadsheets, and database forms. If you use the same document appearance over and over, you should make the document a template containing all the common elements. Then, simply open a new document using the template you've made and much of the work will already be done.

Wizards are Works' way of helping you design a document, spreadsheet, or database from the ground up. You may choose from various designs and features as the Wizard works to produce a finished document with the look you want.

Objectives

- Customize your view of a Works document

- Work with applets, small applications programs that do special jobs

- Use multiple columns

- Insert clipart into your document and have text flow around the pictures

- Use ready-made templates and create your own to automate document creation

- Use Works Wizards to create stylish customized letterheads

Your View of Works

In the next few activities you will create a one-page newsletter for the DSR Corporation. You will add a banner at the top of the page, add a graphic, and use a two-column layout for the text. Until now you have been editing in Normal view. This view is designed for ease of editing and does not show footnotes, headers and footers, or multiple columns. However, if the layout of your page is complex, you might want to see just where each item is placed. To see just how the finished product looks as you edit, Works also provides a page layout view of your page. For everyday work and ease in editing use Normal view; for layout work use Page Layout from the View menu.

You can also enlarge or reduce your view of the document page with the Zoom command. You can zoom from 25 percent (¼X) to 1000 percent (10X) of the normal view so you can see a highly magnified view of a graphic, or the whole page. You can edit at any magnification.

Columns

Works 3.0 lets you use multiple columns in your document. Choose Format, Columns and enter the number of columns you want (text with more than four columns looks a bit tacky). Also choose a value for the space between columns and whether you would like a vertical line separating them. Your entire document must have the same number of columns.

ACTIVITY 6.1

Changing the Number of Columns

1. Open the document NLETTER.WPS from the student diskette.

2. Change your view.

   choose View, Page Layout

   choose View, Zoom

   click the 50% Magnification option button

   click OK

3. Give the document a two-column format.

   choose Format, Columns

type the number **2** *in the* Number of columns *box*

clear the Line between check box if it is marked

click OK

The line between columns only appears in Print Preview and when you print.

4. Compare the Page Layout and Normal views.

choose View, Normal

Only a single column is shown. The paper margins disappear.

choose View, Page Layout

5. Save your work for the next activity.

save your document with the name MYLETTER.WPS

Graphics

Graphics are pictures, graphs, special equations, or anything you insert into a document other than text. Each graphic is inserted within a rectangular frame. In Page Layout view you can size, shape, and move the graphic to any location on the page. You can also flow text around the graphic.

Applets

An applet is a small APPLication program designed to carry out a special task. WordArt is an applet for creating text with a fancy appearance. The text created by WordArt is considered by Works to be a graphic. When you start WordArt you will temporarily leave the Works window and go to the WordArt window with its own menu and icons.

ACTIVITY 6.2

Adding a Title to the Newsletter

1. Be sure MYLETTER.WPS is the active document and prepare to add a title.

   choose View, Page Layout

   choose View, Zoom and set the magnification to 50%

2. Open the WordArt applet.

   press **[CTRL] [HOME]** *to go to the top of the document*

   choose Insert, WordArt

   After a few moments the WordArt window appears. In the following steps, do not click outside the *Enter Your Text Here* box or the menus and Toolbar, or you will be returned to the Works window.

3. Enter and format the title.

   in the Enter Your Text Here *box type* **DSR News of the Month**

   in the Font *list box choose Arial*

   in the Size *box (to the right of the* Font *box), choose Best Fit*

   from the menu choose Format, Shadow

   choose the A with the shadow behind (fourth from the left)

click OK

click the Update Display button in the Enter Your Text Here *dialog box*

click in the document to return to the Works window

4. Save the document and leave it open for the next activity.

Sizing, Shaping, and Moving Graphics

A graphic inserted into a Works document carries a rectangular frame. When the graphic is selected the frame appears as a gray rectangle with eight square handles, four in the corners and one in the middle of each of the four sides. These handles can be used to drag the graphic to a new size and shape. If you drag within the frame you can move the graphic to a new location. To move a graphic you must select the object and then choose Format, Picture/Object. In the *Picture / Object* dialog box click the Text Wrap tab and click the Absolute button. If you choose In-line, the graphic will be treated as a paragraph.

ACTIVITY 6.3

Size and Shape the Title

1. Be sure MYLETTER.WPS is the active document.

2. Prepare to size the title.

    choose View, Zoom and choose a magnification of 75%

    select the title

    choose Format, Picture/Object and click the Text Wrap tab

    click the Absolute button and then click OK

3. Change the view and size the title.

    be sure the title is selected

    move the pointer to the right edge of the graphic and drag the border to the right margin

DSR News of the Month DSR·
PROVIDES·FREE·
MEMBERSHIPS·AT·HEALTH·
CENTER¶

Word Processor

4. Complete the sizing of the title.

drag the bottom center handle down to adjust the graphic

Use the picture below as a guide.

5. Save the document and leave it open for the next activity.

ClipArt

ClipArt refers to previously prepared pictures that you may insert into a Works document. The first time you insert a picture into a document, the ClipArt Gallery accessory program will, if you wish, search your disk and categorize all the pictures it finds. Then when you choose to insert a picture, the Gallery will present clips of your pictures. Double-click the picture you want to insert.

ACTIVITY 6.4

Adding Bullets and ClipArt

1. Be sure MYLETTER.WPS is the active document.

2. Add bullets.

   show the non-printing characters

   select the three paragraphs following the heading Events coming up

   Do not include the blank fourth paragraph.

   click the bullets icon

3. Insert a picture.

   click in front of the paragraph mark above the heading Additional Parking

   choose Insert, ClipArt

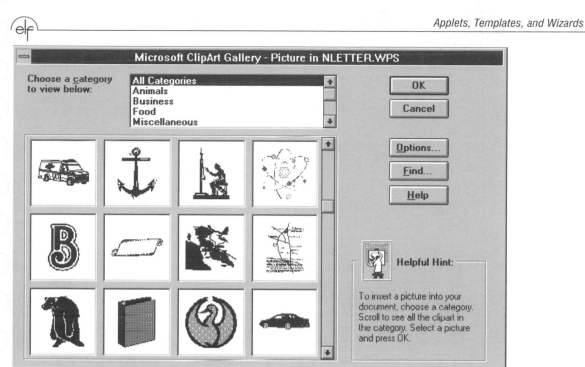

scan the available pictures and choose the blue sedan

click OK

The blue sedan is inserted into the document.

4. Size the picture.

    select the picture

    choose Format, Picture/Object and click the Size tab

    in the scaling options, type 60 into the Width *and* Height *boxes*

    click the Text Wrap tab

    click the In-Line position button

    click OK

5. Position the picture.

    drag the picture above the center of the right column just above the Additional Parking *heading*

    Moving takes a few seconds, so be patient.

6. Format the picture.

    select the picture

    choose Format, Paragraph and click the Breaks and Spacing tab

    add .5 line of spacing Before Paragraph and After Paragraph

7. Save the document and leave it open for the next activity.

Customizing the Toolbar

Perhaps you noticed that the Toolbar shows right, left, and center alignment icons but no icon for justified paragraphs. Perhaps you like to justify your paragraphs and would like to add a suitable icon to the Toolbar. With Works 3.0, you can.

*   Choose Tools, Customize Toolbar.

*   Select the tool category to edit.

*   Drag the tool of your choice from the dialog box to the Toolbar.

*   Drag any tools you don't need from the Toolbar to the dialog box.

*   Press the Reset button to restore the original tools.

Customize Works Toolbar

Select a category to see different sets of buttons. Click on any button to see its description. To add a button, drag it onto the toolbar located at the top of your screen. To remove a button, drag it off the toolbar.

Categories:

File
Edit
View
Insert
Format
Tools
Window

Toolbar Buttons

OK

Cancel

Help

Reset

Choose Reset to revert to default toolbar settings.

Description

Aligns the paragraph at both the left and right indents

☐ Remove **F**ont Name and Point Size from the toolbar.   ☒ E**n**able Tool Tips

elf

ACTIVITY 6.5

Customizing the Works Toolbar

1. Be sure MYLETTER.WPS is the active document.

2. Remove an icon from the Toolbar.

    choose Tools, Customize Toolbar

    drag the Insert Table icon (between the bullet and spell checker icons) from the Toolbar into the dialog box

    The icon disappears.

3. Add the justify alignment icon to the Toolbar.

    in the Customize Works Toolbar *dialog box choose the Format category*

    drag the justify alignment icon (just below the **K** *) to the right of the existing three alignment icons in the Toolbar*

    click OK

4. Use the new icon.

    select the text in the main story (following DSR Provides…)

    click the justify alignment icon

    justify the paragraph about additional parking

5. Save the document and leave it open for the next activity.

Text Flow

You can choose to have text flow around a picture, graph, WordArt, or other object by selecting the object and choosing Format, Picture/Object and clicking the Text Wrap tab. The In-line button will make Works treat the object as if it were a paragraph and you can format the object with space above or below and give the object a left, right, or center alignment. If you choose Absolute text wrap you can drag the object anywhere on the page and text will flow around it.

ACTIVITY 6.6

Formatting an Object with Text Wrap

1. Create a callout.

    make Page Layout your view of the document

    move the insertion to the end of the first paragraph following the word owners

    choose Insert, WordArt

    in the Enter Your Text Here *box type* **We charge by the hour.**

    choose Format, Stretch to Frame so the text will fill the frame

    click in the text area to return to your document

2. Set the text wrap.

    select the WordArt object

    choose Format, Picture/Object and click the Text Wrap tab

    click the absolute button

3. Size and place the callout.

    choose View, Zoom and make the magnification 100%

    be sure the WordArt object is still selected

    drag a right or left handle to make the object the width of a single column

    drag a top or bottom handle to increase the height of the object to the equivalent of 3 lines of text

    drag the callout to the position shown below

4. Save, print, and close the document.

DSR News of the Month

DSR PROVIDES FREE MEMBERSHIPS

Believing that healthy worker are safe and happy worker DSR Corporation has made available a limited number of free one-year memberships at the new WonderBody gym and nutrition center in the Downtown mall. Our reporter recently interviewed the owners.

"We charge by the hour"

Even during a recession people want to stay healthy. There are the finding of Andy Hearty and Nate Hale, owner of the new combination gym and nutrition center in Downtown Mall. "I can't believe how good business has been," said Hale as he shoveled sunflower seeds into a brown paper bag. "I hope it's not just because we're discounting 50% from our usual prices."

His optimism was shared by Hearty who handles the gymnasium end of the business. "You have to eat well and exercise a lot to be healthy like these guys," he said, waving his hand at a group of men and women sweating in and under heavy machines. The gym faintly reminded your reporter of a medieval torture chamber. "Some of them spend all day in here. It's really great. We charge by the hour."

The statistics seem to bear out Hale and Hearty. A report of the National Fitness Association has shown that sales of red meat are down while those of vegetables are on the rise. The chart shows the results.

With better times just around the corner, will the trend continue? Hale and Hearty are betting that it will and DSR is standing by to help.

If you are interested in becoming the one of the lucky owner of a free membership, contact Walter Wing in Travel and Recreation for an application.

Events coming up

- March 14 - First annual younger citizen's walk-a-thon. Join the crowd as they cavort in an exhilarating march around the mall.

- March 18 - Movie classic of the month. 10 cents off on the large box of popcorn with each admission.

- March 21 - Grand opening of Downtown Mall's own photography center. Have your picture taken in black and white.

Additional Parking

The new parking garage behind the WinkleWorm Boutique will be open early next month. The garage will provide parking for an additional fourteen cars. A covered walkway will keep you dry. We respectfully ask that you discontinue parking at the Post Office.

Templates

A template is a model or design for a document, spreadsheet, or database. Every Works document uses a template to define the default environment at the time the document was created. The defaults include margins, fonts, paragraph format, and any other initial parameters necessary to create and edit the document. Works provides several AutoStart templates, or you can create and modify your own. When you create a document from a template the template is not changed.

ACTIVITY 6.7

Using a Works AutoStart Template

1. Prepare to use a template.

    close all open documents

    in the Startup *dialog box click the Use A Template button*

2. Select a template to use.

    in the Choose a template group *box choose AutoStart Personal*

    in the Choose a category *box choose Documents*

    in the Choose a template *box choose Résumé*

3. Select editing options to help you use the template.

    choose Tools, Options

    in the Word Processor area of the dialog box mark Typing replaces selection and Automatic word selection

    Typing replaces selection will enable you to select the template text you want to replace and then type to replace it. Automatic word selection makes it easier to select text to the end of a word.

4. Create your own résumé.

   select Your name *and type your name*

   in turn, select and replace your Street address, City state and zip, *and* Phone number

   under Objective, *select and replace* In this section describe the job… *with the following description*

   I am applying for the position of Administrative Assistant to the Sales Manager of the DSR Corporation in order to make use of my experience in similar positions. I hope to make use of my present computer skills and to enlarge my understanding of product sales.

5. Complete the document.

   insert your own work history, if you wish, or leave the remainder of the document as is

   save the document with the name MYRESUME.WPS

   print the document

6. Close the document.

Creating Your Own Template

You can create and save your own document template. The steps:

- Create a document.

- Add any text and graphics you want to include in the template.

- Change any format settings such as margins and font and size.

- Choose File, Save As and click the Template button. Give the template a name and click OK. The template will be saved in its own directory and will be included in the custom templates list when you choose Use A Template in the *Startup* dialog box.

ACTIVITY 6.8

Creating a Memo Template

1. Create a word processor document.

   show the non-printing characters

2. Add the memo heading.

    press ENTER *to add a blank line at the top of the template*

    type **INTEROFFICE MEMO** *and press* ENTER *3 times to add 2 blank lines*

    select the title and format it with the Arial font, 24 point, bold

    center the title with the Center icon

3. Enter the text for the memo template.

    press CTRL END *to go to the end of the document*

    type **FROM:**

    press TAB *and type* **name of sender**, *press* ENTER *2 times*

    type **TO:**

    press TAB *2 times and type* **name of recipient**, *press* ENTER *2 times*

    type **SUBJECT:**

    press TAB *and type* **subject of memo**, *press* ENTER *2 times*

    type **DATE:**

    press TAB *2 times and type* ***longdate***

    press ENTER *3 times*

    After the two tabs following *DATE:*, use the Insert, Special Character command to insert the Longdate special character.

4. Format the text.

    format the lines From, To, Subject, and Date in Arial, 13 point, bold

5. Choose a default text for the rest of the document.

    press CTRL END *to go to the end of the document*

    choose Format, Font & Style

set the font to Arial, 12 point, plain

Your template should look like the one below.

INTEROFFICE MEMO¶

¶
¶
FROM: →   **name of sender ¶**
¶
TO: → →   **name of recipient¶**
¶
SUBJECT: → **subject of memo¶**
¶
DATE: → → ***longdate*¶**
¶
¶

6. Save the template.

choose File, Save As

click the Template button in the Save As *dialog box*

type **IOMEMO** *in the text box*

click OK to save the template

close the template

Using the Template

1. Create a document from the IOMEMO template.

close any open documents

click the Use A Template button in the Startup *dialog box*

in the Choose a template group *box choose Custom*

in the Choose a category *box choose Custom*

in the Choose a template *box choose IOMEMO*

2. Finish the memo.

    select name of sender

    type your name

    select name of recipient

    type **Walter Wings**

    select subject of memo

    type **Travel Expenses**

    The date is already entered as a special character, ready to be printed.

    press

3. Type the body of the memo:

    Some of our travelers have been late in handing in their travel vouchers. Will you please issue a memo to all employees reminding them of the necessity for promptness in this matter?

    your name

    Travel coordinator

4. Save the memo with the name TEMPMEMO.WPS. Print and close the document.

On Your Own

Create a letterhead template.

1. Open a new document. With the insertion positioned at the top of the page type and center the following letterhead. Format the text to be Times New Roman 10 point, bold.

    DSR Corporation
    1236 Brighton Lane
    Bethesda, MD 22003
    longdate

2. Press [Enter] two times to add two blank lines. Type the words **Body of the letter**.

3. Change the character format to Times New Roman, 12 point, and remove the bold style.

4. Press [Enter] three times and type the following closing. Center the closing.

your name
Director of Activities

5. Save the template with the name LTRHD.

6. Close the document.

7. Create a new document using the template LTRHD.

8. Select the words *Body of the letter* and replace them with:

   The first draft of the annual report will be released next week. Have all department heads review the draft for accuracy and submit any changes before Friday, end of business, next week.

9. Print the report and close the document without saving the changes.

WorksWizards

A WorksWizard provides a quick way to create a specialized finished document. Starting with a document category, the Wizard asks questions and uses your answers to customize the document to your specifications. Wizards work with word processor documents, spreadsheets, and database forms.

ACTIVITY 6.10

Creating a Letterhead with a Wizard

1. Close any open documents.

2. Start the WorksWizard.

   in the Startup *dialog box click the Use A WorksWizard button*

   or

   choose File, WorksWizards

3. Choose a WorksWizard.

   double-click Letterhead

   after reading the information in the first dialog box click the Next button

Word Processor

4. Make your choice of name and address or just art.

To see samples of how the letterhead might look, click each option button.

click the Yes option

click the Next button to go to the next screen

5. Design the letterhead.

click each of the options in turn to view sample letterheads

choose the My Name option button and click the Next button

6. Add your name and address.

add your name, address, city, state, zip, and telephone number to the appropriate text boxes

leave the business text boxes blank and click the Next button

7. Select a letterhead style and line design.

review the styles by clicking each option button in turn

select the Prestige option and click the Next button

pick a line style and click the Next button

8. Add a picture.

review the options

choose the Picture option

click the Next button

choose a top left position for the picture

9. Select a piece of clipart.

choose the clipart option

use the left and right scroll arrows to select a piece of clipart

click the clipart to add it to the letterhead

click Next

10. Let the WorksWizard do the work.

    click the create button and watch the Wizard work

11. Print your letterhead. Save it if you wish.

On Your Own

1. Create your own letterhead with the WorksWizard. Be creative.

2. Save the letterhead as a **template** with the name MYLTMP and close the document.

3. Open the letterhead template and write a letter to your mother.

Quick Check

1. Now that you have used applets, templates, and Wizards, write a sentence describing each.

2. What command lets you enlarge or reduce your page on screen?

3. What is the difference between Normal and Page Layout views?

4. How do you insert clipart into a document? How do you size and shape a picture? How do you move a picture?

5. What are the steps in creating a template?

6. How would you add an icon to the Toolbar?

Part II
The Spreadsheet Program

In This Section

❑ *Start the Spreadsheet program*

❑ *Create, edit, format, and print a spreadsheet*

❑ *Add formulas and functions to a spreadsheet*

❑ *Modify a spreadsheet by adding or deleting rows and columns*

❑ *Create charts from spreadsheet data*

Spreadsheet

Spreadsheet Basics

7

Overview

This chapter will introduce you to the Works 3.0 spreadsheet and how a spreadsheet can work for you. Because Windows programs are designed to use standardized procedures wherever possible, you will find that you already know how to perform many of the basic tasks.

Objectives

- Understand what a spreadsheet is and how it is used

- Start the Works 3.0 spreadsheet

- Identify the parts of the spreadsheet and the program window

- Create a simple spreadsheet

- Save the spreadsheet

- Print the spreadsheet

- Learn some of the rules for entering data into a spreadsheet

What is a "Spreadsheet"?

The term **spreadsheet** applies to data consisting of text and numbers, organized in rows and columns. Before the development of computers, the data was entered onto sheets of ruled paper. If the results of calculations were to be displayed, the calculations were made externally and entered into the spreadsheet. If changes were made, data was erased and reentered manually. Major changes required many recalculations, much erasing, and tedious reentry of data.

Enter the Electronic Spreadsheet

One of the first major uses of computers was the electronic spreadsheet. Although it looked like a paper spreadsheet, the early electronic version made one major improvement—results dependent on new data appeared automatically. Making a change was so easy compared with the paper spreadsheet that you could now use the spreadsheet for "what-if" analysis; that is, how would the results change in a complex spreadsheet if one small factor was changed? The spreadsheet became valuable not only for listing data and its results, but for predictions that would have been too difficult to calculate before.

If you are new to spreadsheets, you can look forward to:

- Typing text and numbers into a convenient grid of rows and columns.

- Making instant calculations by typing in formulas where the results of the calculation are to appear.

- Instant recalculation of results when you change data.

- Using special functions to make complex calculations. Example: a monthly payment based on the amount borrowed, the interest rate, and the length of the loan.

- The benefits of using the mouse and the Windows graphical interface.

- A toolbar to provide quick access to the most frequently used commands.

- Charting functions to provide several types of graphs.

- The same type of thorough on-line help to which you were introduced in the word processor.

Starting the Works 3.0 Spreadsheet Program

You have already learned how to start Works 3.0 and the Works word processor. To start the spreadsheet program, just click the spreadsheet icon in the *Startup* dialog box when Works starts or when you choose File, Create New File from the menu. When you use the spreadsheet program you will see a screen like the one on the next page.

Cell reference area   Enter and Cancel buttons   Formula Bar

Microsoft Works							

File Edit View Insert Format Tools Window Help

Arial   10

B3   X ✓

Sheet1

	A	B	C	D	E	F	G	H
1								
2								
3				Active cell				
4								
5						Column labels		
6								
7		Row labels			Mouse pointer			
8								
9								
10								

Press ENTER, or ESC to cancel.   NUM

Spreadsheet

Many of the parts of the spreadsheet program window area already familiar: the Title, Status, and Menu bars look the same, and the Toolbar is present with some of the usual tools and a few new ones. The mouse pointer has a different shape, however, and the spreadsheet window is certainly different. Here are the new and unfamiliar parts:

Active Cell—The cell where data may be entered or edited. The active cell has a dotted border.

Cell Reference Area—Shows the location of the active cell. The cell reference for the active cell is the intersection of the row and column where the cell lies, with the column value given first.

Mouse Pointer—Has a cross shape in the work area. Takes on other shapes depending on the task you're doing.

Formula Bar—Displays data as you type. The Formula bar is also used for editing data.

Enter and Cancel Buttons—Click these buttons to enter the data into the spreadsheet or to cancel the data entry. The enter button is a check mark and the cancel button an X.

Row and Column Labels—Labels for dividing the spreadsheet into columns and rows. Columns are given alphabetic labels and rows numeric labels.

For the Student New to Spreadsheets

A spreadsheet is arranged as a grid of rows and columns into which you can enter data. The rows are numbered along the left side from 1 to 16,384. Columns are given alphabetic designations starting with A through Z, then AA through AZ, BA through BZ and so on to IV, the 230th column. Wherever a column and row intersect they form a rectangular box called a cell. Each cell has a unique name, or reference, based on the intersection of the column and row that form the cell. The reference of the cell in the upper left corner of the spreadsheet is A1. When a cell is active, as indicated by a heavy border, the reference is shown in the Cell Reference Area at the left end of the Formula bar. The cell is said to be selected.

If you make a mistake while entering data, press the [Backspace] key to erase the last character typed. The text to the right of the insertion point will push aside to make room for the correction. To start over, press [Esc].

Your First Spreadsheet

When you start the spreadsheet program, a new spreadsheet will appear on screen with A1 as the active cell. The temporary name of the spreadsheet in the Title bar is Sheet1. To make a cell active, use the [Right Arrow], [Left Arrow], [Up Arrow], and [Down Arrow] keys to move to the cell, or click the cross-shaped mouse pointer in the cell.

In the next activities you'll start the program and type text and numeric data into the spreadsheet.

ACTIVITY 7.1

Starting the Spreadsheet Program

1. Start Works 3.0 by double-clicking the Microsoft Works icon in the Program Manager.

2. Start the spreadsheet program.

   if the Startup *dialog box appears, click the Spreadsheet button*

   or

if the Startup *dialog box does not appear, choose File, Create New File*

click the Spreadsheet button in the Create, New File dialog box

The spreadsheet program starts and presents you with a new spreadsheet.

ACTIVITY 7.2

Entering Data into the Spreadsheet

1. Use the arrow keys to move to and select the first cell.

    use the arrow keys to move to cell B2

    type **First Quarter Output**

    press ENTER

    Notice that *First Quarter Output* is wider than a single cell. After you press [Enter] the text will spill over into the next cell if it's vacant. If the adjacent cell is not vacant, the text will be truncated (but not lost).

2. Enter the sales regions.

    click cell B5

    type **North** *and press* ↓

    type **South** *and press* ↓

    type **East** *and press* ↓

    type **West** *and press* ENTER

3. Enter the months of the first quarter.

    select cell C4

    type "**Jan** *and press* →

Notice that you were asked to precede the word *Jan* with a double quote. Works makes assumptions about the data as you enter it. For example, typing *Jan* makes Works thinks that you're typing a date rather than text. To override this feature, type a double quote to indicate that you are typing text instead.

type "**Feb** *and press*

type "**Mar** *and press* [ENTER]

4. Add the numeric data.

   enter the numbers so that the spreadsheet looks like the one below

NOTE: As you type into a cell, an X and a check mark appear at the left end of the Formula bar. Clicking the check mark is the same as pressing [Enter]. Clicking the X erases the entry and is the equivalent of pressing [Esc].

	A	B	C	D	E	F
1						
2		First Quarter Output				
3						
4			Jan	Feb	Mar	
5		North	400	435	360	
6		South	380	380	400	
7		East	275	295	280	
8		West	450	455	460	
9						

5. Save the spreadsheet.

   choose File, Save As

   choose the A: drive in the Save As *dialog box*

   type **QSALES** *in the* File Name *text box and click OK*

6. Print the spreadsheet.

   click the Print icon and click OK in the Print *dialog box*

7. Leave the spreadsheet open for the next activity.

Formulas

A formula is a mathematical expression for which you can calculate a result; for instance, =3+4. The result, 7, is displayed in the cell where the formula is typed. A formula always begins with an equal sign to tell Works that the contents of the cell is a formula rather than text.

You can also use cell references in a formula. For example, typing =(A3+A4+A5)/3 in cell A7 would result in the average of the values in cells A3, A4, and A5 being placed in cell A7. The parentheses are necessary so that Works will add the values of the numbers in the three cells before dividing by three to obtain the average. Otherwise, Works would divide A5 by 3 and then add A3 and A4 to the result. You may not use spaces in a formula. If you change the value of one of the cells, the result is immediately recalculated and the new result displayed.

ACTIVITY 7.3

Adding a Formula to the Spreadsheet

1. Add column C.

    click cell B10 and type **Totals**

    click cell C10 and type **=C5+C6+C7+C8**

    press

    The result of the calculation (1505) appears in cell C10. Formulas can be typed in upper or lower case.

Editing Cell Entries

The easiest way to change the contents of a cell is to make the cell active and then type the new contents. To edit the contents of the cell, press [F2] or click where the contents are displayed in the Formula bar. Editing is carried out in the same way as with the word processor.

ACTIVITY 7.4

Editing the Contents of Cells

1. Change a value.

    note the value in C10

type **350** *in cell C7 and press* ENTER

The result in cell C10 immediately changes.

2. Change the title.

    click cell B2

    press F2 *or click at the end of the text in the Formula bar*

    press the ←BACKSPACE *key to delete the word* Output

    type **Sales** *and press* ENTER

3. Save the changes and close the spreadsheet.

On Your Own

1. Create a spreadsheet and type in the data shown below.

	A	B	C	D	E	F
1						
2		Class Grades				
3						
4		Student	Test 1	Test 2	Average	
5		Andy	76	87		
6		Ruth	82	87		
7		John	84	92		
8		Sue	80	85		
9						
10		Average				
11						

2. Type the proper formulas in cells C10, D10, E5, E6, E7, and E8 to produce averages.

    Hint: The formula in C10 would be =(C5+C6+C7+C8)/4. The formula in E7 would be =(C7+D7)/2.

3. Save your work with the name AVERAGES. Print the spreadsheet.

Entering Data into a Spreadsheet

Data that you enter into a spreadsheet can be categorized as either constants or formulas.

Constants—Data consisting of text, numbers, or dates and times that are entered into a spreadsheet and don't change unless you edit the cell in which they reside. Examples:

Mrs. Robinson 32   114A   5-Jan-92

Formulas—A mathematical expression that can consist of values, functions, cell references, and operators that produce a result from data already existing in the spreadsheet. The result of a formula is a numerical value (which may be shown as a date). All formulas begin with the equal (=) sign. Examples:

=3*4   =3.1416*(C4+A2)/D4   =SUM(E6:E12)

Operators—A symbol that indicates a mathematical operation. In the expression 5*3, the "*" is an operator indicating that 5 is to be multiplied by 3. The Works arithmetic operators:

#2

+	addition
-	subtraction
*	multiplication
/	division
%	percentage
^	exponentiation

Precedence—When a formula is entered into a cell, precedence determines the order in which operations will be carried out to calculate the result. Works always performs arithmetic operations in a certain order. The order of precedence or evaluation is shown below:

-	negation; indicates a negative value such as -32
%	the value is changed to a percentage (divided by 100)
^	exponentiation
* and /	multiplication and division
+ and -	addition and subtraction

Precedence can be altered using parentheses around operations that are to be carried out first.

Spreadsheet

Examples:

Formula	Result
=3+5*2	3+10 = 13
=(3+5)*2	(8)*2 = 16
=8+10/2+4	8+5+4 = 17
=(8+10)/(2+4)	(18)/(6) = 3

When the precedence of operators is equal, operations are carried out from left to right.

Example:

=27/9/3 from left to right: 27/9 = 3, then 3/3 = 1

Numbers, Text, Dates, and Times—As you enter data into a spreadsheet, Works will classify the data as either numeric or text. Data that can be operated on mathematically is considered numeric; other data is considered text. Dates, such as *Jan* (understood by Works to be 1 Jan of the current year) in your first spreadsheet, are kept by Works as numbers (the number of days since 1/1/1900), but are usually displayed as text.

Numeric examples:

    32   21,459 $45.22   36%   -11   3.164E6

You may use the +, -, ( ), $, %, and E or e as a part of a number. Enter a negative value by preceding the number with a "-", or if it's in a currency format enclosing it with parentheses. E or e are used to enter numbers in scientific notation; 3.164E6 is the same as 3,164,000. Numeric values are usually aligned against the right edge of a cell. Works removes extraneous significant figures to the right of the decimal point; entering 2.00 will result in the number 2 appearing in the active cell. Later, you will learn to format numbers with the desired number of significant figures.

Text examples:

    Joe   A22   16 Loric Lane   3*4   "36

The first three examples are considered text because they cannot be parts of a mathematical expression. The fourth example, 3*4, is considered text because it does not have an = sign in front to tell Works to carry out the indicated operation. The final example will result in the numerals 36 being placed in a cell. The double quote is required so that Works will convert what it would normally consider a value, into text. Text is normally aligned against the left margin of a cell. Notice that after you have entered the text into a cell, a double quote appears at the left end of the text in the Formula bar, but not in the cell.

Date and time examples:

> January   7/23/92   3:50pm   July 23, 1992   July 4

All dates are stored by Works as consecutive whole numbers. Times are stored as the decimal part of a day.

The series of dates begins with 1 Jan, 1900, which is day 1.

- 15 Jan, 1900, is day 15

- 1 Feb, 1900, is day 32

- 23 July, 1992, is day 33808

Noon on 23 July, 1992, entered as *7/23/92 12:00*, is kept by Works as day 33808.5 By recording dates and times as numbers, Works calculates the period between two dates. You can use either a slash (/) or a hyphen (-) as a separator in dates. Whether the date appears as text or a number depends on the way it is formatted, a subject you will explore in a later chapter.

In the next activity you will create a spreadsheet and practice entering data.

● ■ ACTIVITY 7.5
● Entering Data

1. Close any open spreadsheets and create a new one.

    choose File, Close

    or

    double-click the spreadsheet Control-menu box

    choose File, Create New File

    click the Spreadsheet button

2. Enter the following formulas and observe the results in the spreadsheet. Try to calculate the results in your head first. Type each formula in a different cell.

=3+5/2

=(3+5)/2

=8+10/2+4

=(8+10)/(2+4)

=3^2

=2^.5

The last two formulas use exponentiation. 3^2 is 3 to the second power or 3*3. The last formula calculates the square root of 2 or 2 to the .5 power, 1.4142136.

3. Enter the following numbers into the spreadsheet and observe the results.

32

21,000

21234

$45.00

45.00

36.2%

3E3

The number 3E3 or 3.00E+03 means $3*10^3$, or 3,000.

4. Enter the following text into the spreadsheet and observe the results.

Jack Robinson

A64

303 South Cornell Circle

3+5

"21

"Jan

5. Enter the following dates and times into the spreadsheet and observe the results.

    3/9/91

    10:32pm

    Jan

    July 14

    Jan 16, 1993

    Each entry aligns against the right edge of the cell. This tells you that Works considers them numbers. The last entry resulted in a series of pound signs, "########". This means that the numeric entry is too wide to fit into the cell. To widen the column, choose Format, Column Width and type in a number to make the column wider. Use the value 20 to double the width of the column.

6. Close the spreadsheet without changes unless you're going to do the next On Your Own.

Clearing Cell Entries

To clear or delete a cell entry, select the cell, then choose Edit, Clear.

On Your Own

1. In a blank cell, type a formula that will calculate the number of minutes in a year.

2. In a blank cell, type a formula that will calculate the discounted price on a book. The original price is $13.95 and the discount 15 percent. The discounted price is found by subtracting 0.15 from 1.00 (1.00-.15), and multiplying the result (0.85) times the original price. Note that you cannot use a $ sign in a formula.

3. In a blank cell, type a formula that will calculate the weekly pay a person would receive if they were paid $5.50 per hour and worked 40 hours.

4. Type the values $34.24 in cell G4, $98.22 in H4 and $55.67 in cell I4. In cell K4 enter a formula that will add the values together. In cell L4 enter a formula that will calculate their average.

5. Close the spreadsheet and do not save the changes.

Ranges

A **range** is a rectangular group of selected cells that appear highlighted on the screen. The range may be as small as a single cell or as large as the entire spreadsheet. Once a range has been selected, a command will apply to the entire range. The techniques for selecting a range are similar to those for selecting text in the word processor.

- A range can be selected by dragging the mouse pointer from the center of the cell at the beginning of the range, called the anchor cell, to the cell at the end of the range. A selected range appears highlighted, except for the anchor cell. Drag from the center of the cell, not the border.

- With the keyboard you can select the anchor cell and then hold down [Shift] and use the arrow keys to select the range.

- With either method, the anchor cell becomes active.

- To deselect the range, click somewhere in the spreadsheet or press one of the arrow keys.

- A range may be specified by the cell references of any two opposite corners separated by a colon; for example, B3:D6 is a range with its upper left corner in cell B3 and its lower right corner in D6.

- To select an entire spreadsheet, click the blank rectangle at the intersection of the spreadsheet row and column labels.

In the next activity you will first open an existing spreadsheet from the student diskette and save it by a different name. The steps for opening and saving files are the same as for the word processor except the spreadsheet program uses the extension .WKS for file names.

ACTIVITY 7.6
Selecting a Range

1. Open the spreadsheet RANGES.WKS from the student diskette.

   choose File, Open Existing File

   choose the A: drive in the Drives *box*

   scroll through the File Name *list box and double-click the file RANGES.WKS*

2. Save the file with a new name.

   choose File, Save As and type **MYRANGES** *in the* File Name *text box* *click OK to save the file*

3. Select the range C9:E9 containing the number 1.

    point to cell C9

    drag the mouse pointer to E9

4. Select the range A10:A16.

    click cell A10

    hold down **SHIFT** *and press* **↓** *6 times*

5. Choose a range using the [F8] function key.

    click cell G2, then press **F8**

    click cell H14 to select the range G2:H14

6. Clear a range.

    select the range B3:D6

    choose Edit, Clear

7   Undo the clear.

    choose Edit, Undo Clear

    Works 3.0 has an Undo command in the Edit menu.

8. Clear the rest of the ranges so that you have a blank spreadsheet.

Entering Data into a Range

Data entry can often be simplified by selecting a range first. After the range is selected, type the data into the anchor (active) cell and press [Enter] or click the check box in the Formula bar when you finish. The data is entered and the next cell becomes active. Repeat the process for the remaining cells.

You can also fill a range with a value. Type the value in the anchor cell, then press [Ctrl] [Enter].

ACTIVITY 7.7

Using Ranges to Enter Data

1. Use the blank MYRANGES.WKS spreadsheet for this activity.

2. Select the range B3:C5.

   point to cell B3

   drag the pointer to cell C5

3. Enter a list of names and values into the range.

   type **Wilson** *and press* ⏎ENTER

   type **Sims** *and press* ⏎ENTER

   type **Brown** *and press* ⏎ENTER

   type **75** *and press* ⏎ENTER

   type **82** *and press* ⏎ENTER

   type **91** *and press* ⏎ENTER

   press → *to deselect the range*

4. Fill a range with the same value.

   select the range E4:G11

   type your first name into E4, the active cell

   press CTRL ⏎ENTER

5. Clear the spreadsheet.

   choose Edit, Select All

   choose Edit, Clear

   click a cell to remove the highlight

Creating a Series by Filling

Many spreadsheets use a series of dates, times, or numbers as row or column headings. The Works spreadsheet program can create a variety of these series if you suggest the first member and the interval between members of the series. For example, you might want the months that run from Jan. 92 to Dec. 92. To create such a series, type the first member of the series in the cell where the series is to start, then drag through the range where you want the series to appear. Next, choose Edit, Fill Series and in the *Fill Series* dialog box choose a series type and step. You must use a number or a date with a fill series.

Examples are given below.

First Cell	Units	Steps by	Result
Jan	Month	1	January, February, March
January	Month	3	January, April, July
January 3, 1992	Day	1	January 3, 1992, January 4, 1992
3	Number	3	3, 6, 9
25	Number	-5	25, 20, 15
3/2/92	Year	1	3/2/92, 3/2/93, 3/2/94
2/28/92	Day	1	2/28/92, 2/29/92, 3/1/92
2/28/92	Weekday	1	2/28/92, 3/2/92, 3/3/92 The 29th and 1st are on the weekend.

ACTIVITY 7.8
Creating a Series by Filling

1. Select and clear the spreadsheet.

   click the rectangle in the upper-left corner of the spreadsheet at the intersection of the spreadsheet column and row headings

   choose Edit, Clear

2. Create a monthly series.

   *type **Jan** in cell B3*

drag the pointer across to cell E3 to select the range B3:E3

choose Edit, Fill Series

mark Month in the Units *box and type* **3** *in the* Step By *box*

click OK to fill the range

3. Add a number series.

    type **1** *in cell A4*

    drag the selection down to cell A34

    choose Edit, Fill Series

    mark Number in the Units *box and type* **1** *in the* Step By *box*

    click OK to fill the range

4. Close the spreadsheet and do not save the changes.

Functions

You've already used several formulas for calculating the results of mathematical expressions. A function is a special type of a formula for use where a normal formula might be too lengthy, as in adding a long column of numbers. Another use for a function is where you may not know how to write a formula to make the calculation you want, like figuring your monthly car or house payment.

A function might be thought of as a formula that asks a question and returns an answer. A function had two parts: a name and a set of arguments contained in parentheses. An argument is information that is given the function so it can do its job. Some functions require a single argument, or none, while some require several arguments. An argument can be a range, a cell address, or a value.

Here are some simple functions:

Function	Result
=SUM(A1:A10)	the sum of the values in the range A1:A10
=AVG(C9:G9)	the average of the values in the range C9:G9
=SQRT(13)	the square root of 13
=SQRT(C3)	the square root of the value in cell C3

ACTIVITY 7.9

Using Functions in a Spreadsheet

1. Create a spreadsheet.

2. Type the following data into the spreadsheet range B2:B10, one value in each cell, starting with cell B2.

   345, **621**, **816**, **733**, **490**, **322**, **555**, **690**, **421**

3. Enter the SUM function.

   type **Sum** *in cell A12*

   in cell B12 type **=SUM(B2:B10)**

   press ENTER

4. Enter the AVG function and select the range with the mouse.

   type **Average** *in cell A13*

   type **=AVG(** *in cell B13*

   drag the mouse through the range B2:B10

   As you move through the selection, the Formula bar shows the selected range.

   type **)** *to close the parentheses*

   press ENTER

5. Enter the MAX function and select the range with the keyboard.

   type **Maximum** *in cell A14*

   type **=MAX(** *in cell B14*

   use *to move to cell B10*

   hold down **SHIFT** *and use* ↑ *to extend the range to cell B2*

   type **)** *and press* ENTER

6. Leave the spreadsheet open for the next activity.

Spreadsheet

Using the Sum Icon in the Toolbar

The Sum icon provides an easy way to sum the values in a column or row. The Sum icon has the Greek letter sigma (Σ) on its face. Click on the cell below a column of numbers or to the right of a row of numbers where you want the sum to appear. Click the Sum icon and Works inserts the SUM function with the range already in place. If Works has chosen the correct range press [Enter], or click the check mark in the Formula bar, to insert the sum into the selected cell.

ACTIVITY 7.10

Adding with the Sum Icon

1. Clear the SUM function from cell B12.

    click cell B12

    choose Edit, Clear

2. Use the Sum icon to total the column.

    make sure cell B12 is selected

    click the Sum icon

    press

3. Enter the following values.

    type **234** *in cell D8*

    type **331** *in cell E8*

    type **455** *in cell F8*

4. Sum the cells.

    click in cell H8

    click the Sum icon

    press

5. Close the spreadsheet and do not save the changes.

Formulas and Pointing

In previous activities you learned how to type formulas that included cell references. Many times you will be working in areas of the spreadsheet that are away from the row and column headings or your spreadsheets may cover more than one screen. In these cases you may find it difficult to choose the correct cell references. To overcome this difficulty, Works allows you to point to the cells you want to include in a formula using either the mouse or the keyboard. If you take the time to learn this technique, you may find yourself using it as your preferred method.

1. **Mouse**—Click the cell where the result of the formula is to be displayed.

   Keyboard—Use the arrow keys to move to the cell where the result is to be displayed.

2. **Mouse and Keyboard**—Type the equal sign (=) to tell Works that a formula is being entered.

3. **Mouse**—Click on the first cell to be entered into the formula, or type in a number that is to be included in the formula.

   Keyboard—Use the arrow keys to move to the first cell, or type in a number that is to be included in the formula.

   The cell address or number appears in the formula bar.

4. **Mouse or Keyboard**—Type an operator (+, -, /, *, or ^).

5. Repeat steps 3 and 4 until the final cell reference or number has been entered.

6. Press [Enter].

As an example, the formula =A4+D4 could be entered into cell F4 with the mouse or keyboard following these steps:

Mouse	**Keyboard**
click on cell F4	move to cell F4
type =	type =
click cell A4	move to cell A4
type +	type +
click on cell D4	move to cell D4
press [Enter]	press [Enter]

Spreadsheet

ACTIVITY 7.11

Entering a Formula by Pointing

1. Create a spreadsheet.

2. Enter data for use by a formula.

    type **321** *in cell B2*

    type **416** *in cell G3*

    type **211** *in cell A9*

    type **555** *in cell H12*

    type **3** *in cell D6*

3. Use pointing to enter the formula **=(B2+G3+A9+H12)*D6** in cell D10. Watch the Formula bar as you type.

    click cell D10 and type **=(**

    click cell B2 and type **+**

    click on cell G3 and type **+**

    click on cell A9 and type **+**

    click on cell H12 and type **)***

    click on cell D6 and press [ENTER]

4. Clear the formula from cell D10 and reenter the formula using pointing and the keyboard.

5. Close the spreadsheet and do not save the changes.

Formulas and Circular References

A **circular reference** occurs when a formula makes reference to itself. For example, if the range for the SUM function includes the cell where the function resides, the sum will be included in the calculation. This causes the value in the cell to change and the function to recalculate. This causes the value in the cell to change again and the function to recalculate again, and so on. At this point Works will show the word *CIRC* in one of the boxes along the right end of the Status bar. You must correct the range used by the function so that it doesn't include the cell in which the function is entered. Works doesn't issue a warning other than the message in the Status bar. Be careful—a circular error will give an incorrect answer!

On Your Own

1. Create a spreadsheet and the following series:

    Yearly from Jan 1, 1980, through Jan 1, 1994.

    Numbers starting with 100 and decreasing to 0 in steps of 10.

    Starting with April 1 and going weekly through the end of June
    Hint: Use April 1 as a start, Day as a unit, and 7 as the increment.

2. Sum the numbers from 1 through 99 by using a fill series and the SUM function.

3. Make a table of the square roots of the numbers between 0 and 20. The square root function is =SQRT( ).

4. Clear your spreadsheet. In cell C2 enter 14. In cell C3 enter 18. In cell C4 enter 22.

    In C6 type the formula **=SUM(C2:C6)**. What does the Works spreadsheet program have to say? Look at the right end of the Status bar. Does the sum function give the correct answer? Correct the formula to read **=SUM(C2:C5)**. Does the error message disappear. Do you now have the correct answer?

5. Look up the term **circular reference** using Help.

6. Close all spreadsheets without saving changes.

Quick Check

1. What two types of data can you enter into a spreadsheet?

    formulas & information

2. What are the mathematical operators used in the spreadsheet program?

    p129

Spreadsheet

3. Evaluate the following formulas the way Works will.

=(5+3)*(4+2)/4   equals   *12*

(8)*(6)/4
48/4
12

=5+3*4-2/4   equals   *15*

5+12-2/4
5+12 - 2
17-2 15

4. What are two ways to select a range of cells?

1. *arrow keys*
2. *mouse*

5. How do you erase or clear the contents of a range?

delete

6. What character must you always use to precede a formula?

equal sign

7. You would like to sum the subtotals in cells B6, B14, and B29 with the result in cell in B40. Describe how you would use pointing with either the mouse or keyboard to create a formula for the sum of the three values.

= B6+ B14 + B29 ⇐ formula
click | put in cell B40 then enter

8. What is a circular reference?

P(42)

Editing and Formatting

8

Overview

Spreadsheets are dynamic rather than static. You will find yourself constantly adding, deleting, moving, and copying data as your spreadsheet changes and additional data becomes available. You will also want to format the spreadsheet, choosing the best way to display numbers and dates and using bold, italic, and underline as you did with the word processor. In this chapter you will learn the basics of spreadsheet editing and formatting and how to manage larger jobs with minimum effort.

Objectives

- Insert cells, columns, and rows

- Move and copy text and values

- Move and copy formulas

- Distinguish between absolute and relative copying

- Use an input cell

- Format numbers and dates to display information the way you want

- Change column widths

- Format with bold, italic, underline, and fonts

Editing the SPECIAL CITIES Spreadsheet

Learning to edit a spreadsheet consists of mastering a variety of simple tasks like widening a column to fit its contents, copying a formula into a range of cells, or inserting a blank row so that a new item can be added. You will learn about these topics and others by editing a simple spreadsheet.

Spreadsheet

Inserting Rows

When you open the next spreadsheet you will notice that there are five cities in it. A sixth city needs to be added as row 6. A row is added across the entire width of the spreadsheet and pushes down the already existing row and all the rows below it. To select a row, click the row label at the left edge of the spreadsheet window. To insert more than one row, drag the pointer through the row labels to select the desired number. When you insert row 6, the data beginning with Utica will push down and become row 7.

ACTIVITY 8.1

Inserting a Row

1. Open the spreadsheet SCITY.WKS from the student diskette.

2. Select row 6.

    click the number 6 in the row labels

3. Insert a row.

    choose Insert, Row/Column

4. Add the data.

    type **Austin** *in cell A6*

    type **Texas** *in cell B6*

    type **90.2** *in cell C6*

    type **301000** *in cell D6*

Inserting Columns

The column is added to the entire height of the spreadsheet. Select the column by clicking on the column heading. As the column is added, the existing column and all columns to the right are pushed to the right.

ACTIVITY 8.2

Inserting a Column

1. Select the column.

click the column heading A

2. Insert the column.

   choose Edit, Insert Row/Column

3. Add the numbers to the rows.

   type 1 in cell A3

   select the range A3:A8

   choose Edit, Fill Series and choose number units and step by 1

   click OK

4. Add two more rows.

   add rows above and below the title, Six Special Cities

NOTE: You can also add a row or column if only a single cell is selected. However, in this case you must tell Works whether you want to add a row or a column, thus adding an extra step.

Changing Column Widths and Row Heights

Columns B and C in the spreadsheet are not wide enough to display the full names of the cities and states and column A is much wider that it needs to be. You can change column widths with the mouse or by using the Format, Column Width command.

Column Width—The default column width for a new spreadsheet is 10. To set a column to the best fit for the longest data in it, mark the Best Fit check box.

If you want to change the width of individual columns, select the columns by clicking or dragging in the column labels (or select cells in those columns), then type a number in the *Column Width* text box.

Mouse—If you move the mouse pointer into the column labels it will change to a vertical line with arrows pointing left and right as the pointer crosses the boundary between columns. You can then drag the pointer to the desired width.

You can also set the column for the best fit to the data. In the column labels double-click on the boundary between columns.

Row Height—The row height command changes the height of a selected row. You can use either the menu or the mouse in the same way that you did for column widths.

ACTIVITY 8.3

Changing the Width of a Column

1. Select column A.

    click on the column label A

2. Change the width.

    choose Format, Column Width

    type **3** *in the* Column Width *text box and click OK*

3. Change the width of column B.

    click the right edge of the column B label where the pointer changes to a vertical line with left- and right-pointing arrows

    drag the edge of the column to the right

    experiment with the width until San Francisco *shows in its entirety*

    select the column B label

    choose Format, Column Width to see the actual width of column B

4. Change the width of columns C through F.

    double-click the boundary between columns C and D for a best fit for column C

    using your choice of method to change the column widths of the remaining columns

    What happens if you set column A for best fit?

5. Save the spreadsheet with a new name.

    choose File, Save As

    be sure that the A: drive is selected in the Drives *box*

    type **MYCITY** *in the* File Name *text box*

press [ENTER]

6. Close the spreadsheet.

CAUTION: It is a good idea to save your spreadsheets frequently to avoid losing your work if power is interrupted. It is also wise to save just before you do something major to the spreadsheet. In this way you will have a backup copy if you make a bad mistake. If you do make a mistake, close the spreadsheet and do not save the changes. Then open the previous version from disk. You can save your work in just seconds by pressing [Ctrl] [S]. You can also save several versions of the spreadsheet with different names as you continue to edit and refine your work.

Moving and Copying

You can move and copy both data and formulas in Works spreadsheets, but the results depend on what you are moving and copying. If you move text or numbers, then the text and numbers appear in their new location. With formulas, however, something more is involved. Suppose you moved the contents of cells A1, B1, and C1 to A4, B4, and C4 as in the spreadsheet below.

In cells A4 and B4, you would want to find 32 and 37, respectively. But in Cell C4 you would want to find =A4+B4 instead of =A1+B1. The spreadsheet program understands this and when you move or copy a formula, the formula is changed relative to the difference between its old and new locations. This is called relative moving and copying using relative cell references.

	A	B	C
1	32	37	=A1+B1
2			
3			
4	32	37	=A4+B4
5			

Moving

You can move data with the Edit, Cut and Paste commands from the menu or by dragging and dropping with the mouse as you did with the word processor.

Spreadsheet

Keyboard—Select the data range you want to move. Choose the Edit, Cut command to move the selected data to the clipboard. Select the destination. If you are moving a range, it is only necessary to select the upper left corner of the destination. Choose Edit, Paste to paste the data into its new location.

Mouse—Select the data range you want to move. Move the mouse pointer to one of the borders of the range where the pointer changes from an open cross to the drag pointer. Drag the range to a new location.

Clipboard—The Clipboard is an area of memory where selected data is placed temporarily during a cut or copy operation. The Paste command retrieves the contents of the clipboard and inserts it at the position of the selected cell in the spreadsheet. Only the data from the latest cut or copy remains in the Clipboard.

ACTIVITY 8.4
Moving Data

1. Open the spreadsheet COPY.WKS from the student diskette.

2. Move the range F10:H12.

    select the range F10:H12

    choose Edit, Cut

    select the cell G15

    choose Edit, Paste

3. Move the range back with the mouse.

    select the range G15:I17

    move the pointer to the upper border where it becomes the drag pointer

    drag the range back to F10:H12 (upper left cell of range is at F10)

ACTIVITY 8.5
Making a Relative Move

1. Note the formula in cell C1.

    click cell C1

    note the contents in the Formula bar

2. Move the range A1:C1 to A4:C4.

   select the range A1:C1

   drag the range down four rows to A4:C4

3. Note the formula in cell C4.

   click cell C4

   note in the Formula bar that the formula has changed

Copying

In some ways, copying is like moving. You select a range and copy its contents somewhere else. But you can do more than that. Many times you'll want to copy a range into a larger range, and this makes copying one of the most important spreadsheet tasks to master. It is so important that Works uses two special commands in addition to Copy—Fill Down and Fill Right.

- To copy a range, select the range and choose Edit, Copy. Then click on the cell in the upper left corner of the intended destination range and choose Edit, Paste. You can also copy a single cell into a range by selecting the cell and choosing Edit, Copy. Then select the range that the cell is to be copied into and choose Edit, Paste. Formulas will be copied relatively.

- To fill a range, select the cell at the top or left end of the range. Drag from that cell through the range you wish to fill (copying from the anchor cell into the range) and choose Edit, Fill Down or Edit, Fill Right.

ACTIVITY 8.6

Copying a Formula

1. Be sure COPY.WKS is the active spreadsheet.

2. Enter a formula to copy.

   click cell B19

   click the Sum icon and press **ENTER** *to sum the column*

3. Copy the formula into the other two columns.

   drag through the range B19:D19

   choose Edit, Fill Right

Spreadsheet

4. Check the copied formulas to see if they are correct.

5. Copy text into a range.

   type your first name into cell A8

   drag through the range A8:A12

   choose Edit, Fill Down to copy your name into the range

6. Close the spreadsheet and do not save the changes.

On Your Own

1. Open the spreadsheet MYCITY.WKS. If you did not complete your work in MYCITY.WKS, open MYCITYCA.WKS instead.

2. Type the word **Total** in cell C12. Write a formula or function to add the areas in column D and have the sum appear in cell D12.

3. Use the Fill Right or Edit, Copy and Paste commands to copy the formula into E12.

4. The population density equals the Population divided by the Area. Type a formula in cell F5 to calculate the population density. Copy the formula into cells F6:F10 using the method of your choice.

5. Save and close the spreadsheet.

Absolute vs. Relative References

In the previous activities, formulas containing cell references that were copied have been adjusted by Works to match their locations. If a formula in row A concerned cells in row A, then copying that formula to row B would result in a formula that concerned cells in row B. This is called relative copying and the formulas contain relative references.

On many occasions, however, you may want to copy a formula without changing the cell references. An example might be where formulas that are copied make use of the value in one particular cell, called an input cell. Copying where addresses do not change is called absolute copying and the formulas involved contain an absolute reference.

In order to characterize a cell address in a formula as absolute, precede the column and row numbers with a dollar sign, for example, C12. When this reference is copied, it remains C12.

In the next activity, you will open a spreadsheet, create an input cell, and copy formulas containing absolute references.

Activity 8.7

Entering Absolute References

1. Open the spreadsheet COPY.WKS from the student diskette.

2. Label the input cell.

   type **Input** *in cell E1*

   type **10** *in cell E2*

3. Write a formula to add the range F2:F4 and multiply it by the value in the input cell.

   in cell F5, type **=SUM(F2:F4)*E2**

   The result should be 130.

4. Copy the formula into the range G5:H5.

   drag through the range F5:H5

   choose Edit, Fill Right

5. Examine the results. Check the formulas in cells G5 and H5. Note that the copied formulas do not refer to the input cell E2.

6. Correct the formulas to make use of the input cell.

   type **=SUM(F2:F4)*E2** *in cell F5*

7. Copy the corrected formula into the range.

   drag through the range F5:H5

   choose Edit, Fill Right

8. Examine the results. Again, check the formulas in cells G5 and H5. Note that the copied formulas now refer to the input cell.

9. Change the value in the input cell.

   type **3** *in cell E2*

   Note that all three values in the range F5:H5 have changed to their expected values.

10. Leave the spreadsheet open if you plan to do the next On Your Own. Otherwise, close the spreadsheet without saving any changes.

On Your Own

1. In the above activity, both the row and column (E2) were made absolute references.

2. Repeat steps 6 through 8 using the formula =SUM(F2:F4)*$E2. Does this work as well? Why?

3. Repeat steps 6 through 8 using the formula =SUM(F2:F4)*E$2. Does this work as well? Why?

4. Close the spreadsheet without saving the changes.

5. Here's a challenge. Create a multiplication table like the one shown below. First type the row and column headings, 1 through 10 for each. Change the column widths to 5 so the entire table is shown within the window. Then in cell C3 type a formula that multiplies the row and column number to give the product (the formula shown will only work for that single cell, and filling it down or to the right will give incorrect results). The formula will contain mixed cell references, that is, part of the cell reference will be absolute and the other part relative, for example, $R4 or G$15. Select the range C3:L12. Fill the formula down into the range C3:C12 and then, without deselecting the range, fill right into the remainder of the range. If you have the correct formula in cell C3 all the formulas filled into the remaining 99 cells will be correct.

	A	B	C	D	E	F	G	H	I	J	K	L
1			1	2	3	4	5	6	7	8	9	10
2												
3	1		=C1*A3									
4	2											
5	3											
6	4											
7	5											
8	6											
9	7											
10	8											
11	9											
12	10											
13												

Case Study

In this case study you will open a spreadsheet from the student diskette and add formulas to calculate labor costs. The spreadsheet could be used for "what-if" analysis of the effects of changes in Indirect, G&A, and Overhead rates on the total hourly cost of labor.

1. Open the spreadsheet LABOR.WKS from the student diskette.

2. Insert a row at the current row 2, under the title *Labor Rates*.

3. Insert a row at the current row 5, above the name *Smith, John*.

4. In cell D6, Indirect Labor for John Smith, type the formula **=C6*G13**. This formula is taken from the instructions in cell B13; the indirect labor equals the direct labor multiplied by the indirect rate. You must use a relative reference when referring to cell C6 because you want to be able to copy the formula into the next two rows and have the reference change accordingly. You must use an absolute reference for the indirect rate in cell G13 because you want the indirect rate input cell to be referenced by formulas that have been copied.

5. In cell E6, type a formula based on the instructions in cell B14.

6. In cell F6, type a formula based on the instructions in cell B15.

7. In cell G6, type a formula based on the instructions in cell B16.

8. Copy the formulas in C6:G6 into the two rows below.

9. In cell G10, type a formula that will total the labor costs in column G. Write down the total.

10. Change the G&A rate to 60 percent by typing **60%** in cell G14. Which cells are affected by the change? What is the new total?

11. Add a line at row 9, then add an employee, **Alton, Sue**, with an hourly rate of **$4.87**. Fill the formulas into the range D9:G9. Hint: select C9:G9 and use Fill Down. (You may have to change the range for the formula in cell G11). What is the new total?

12. Experiment with different values in the input cells to see how changes in rates affect the total.

13. Add serial numbers in column A for the four names.

14. Save the spreadsheet with the new name MYLABOR.WKS. Close the spreadsheet.

Formatting

The appearance of your finished spreadsheet often has as much impact on the reader as the data it contains. A spreadsheet becomes more readable and usable if headings are clearly marked, important data is enhanced, and borders enclose similar data. Numerical data should show the correct number of significant figures with dollar signs and other characters as appropriate. This is called formatting, changing the appearance of a spreadsheet without changing the actual content, and it is an important part of spreadsheet preparation.

Every cell has a format. As you type in text or a number, the spreadsheet program assigns a general format based on the data being entered. If you enter text, the text aligns against the left edge of the cell. If you type in numbers, the numbers align against the right edge of the cell. The formatting can be changed to whatever you think best for clarity and legibility.

Alignment

By default, the spreadsheet program aligns text against the left edge of the cell and numbers against the right edge of the cell. This is called General alignment. You can also choose to align either text or numbers in the right, left, or center of a cell using the Format, Alignment command or by clicking one of the alignment icons on the Toolbar.

To align data, select the range, then choose Format, Alignment and select an option button in the Alignment area. You can also choose to align vertically within a cell.

In the next activity you will open the MYCITY.WKS spreadsheet and align the column headings and the title. If you did not finish your earlier work on this spreadsheet, open the MYCITYFO.WKS spreadsheet instead.

ACTIVITY 8.8
Aligning Text

1.   Open the MYCITY.WKS (or MYCITYFO.WKS) spreadsheet.

2.   Select a range.

     select the range B4:F4

3.   Align the text.

     choose Format, Alignment

     click the Center option button

     click OK

Alignment Icons

You can also align text or numbers with the alignment icons on the Toolbar.

ACTIVITY 8.9

Using the Alignment Icons

1. Practice alignment with the alignment icons.

    select the range B5:B10

    click the Right alignment icon

    click the Center alignment icon

    click the Left alignment icon

NOTE: You can also align numbers to the left, right, or center, although this is usually reserved for special cases. Right alignment is the only type that will align decimal points properly.

Character Formatting

If you look in the Toolbar you will recognize *Font* and *Size* text boxes similar to those introduced with the word processor. The default font is MS Sans Serif. All the fonts and styles that you choose are applied to an entire cell or range. You cannot change the format for a part of a single cell.

CAUTION: If you change fonts, you may not be able to find the default font in the fonts list when you want to change back Type **MS Sans Serif** in the *Font* box to restore the default font.

ACTIVITY 8.10

Applying Character Formatting

1. Format the title of the spreadsheet.

    select the title, SIX SPECIAL CITIES

    choose Times New Roman from the Font *list box*

    choose 14 from the Size *list box*

    click the Bold icon on the Toolbar

    Note that the row height changes to accommodate the larger font size.

2. Leave the spreadsheet open for the next activity.

Formatting Numbers

Formatting numbers consists of two parts:

- First, the type of format such as currency, percentage, with commas or without.

- Second, the number of significant figures that will be displayed to the right of the decimal point.

In a new spreadsheet, numbers are formatted with a General format by default. This format will display a number with as much accuracy as possible consistent with the width of the cell. To give a number a different format choose Number and click the option you want.

All other formats have a default of two significant figures to the right of the decimal.

- **Fixed** format displays a number with a leading minus if the number is negative and a decimal point. Examples: 65478.23 and -65478.23.

- **Currency** format shows a $ sign leading the number and commas every three significant figures. A negative value is enclosed in parentheses or can be show in red. Examples: $1,234.56 and ($1,234.56).

- **Comma** format displays a number with a comma occurring every three significant figures to the left of the decimal. Parentheses are shown around negative numbers or can be shown in red. Examples: 65,478.23 and (65,478.23).

- **Percent** format shows a % sign trailing the number. A minus sign is placed before negative numbers. 12.32% and -12.32% are examples. Remember the value 8.32 is 832% and 5% is 0.05.

- **Exponential** or **scientific notation** format is used for very large and very small numbers. It consists of a value with one significant figure to the left of the decimal and a multiplier that is a multiple of 10. Examples of exponential formatting:

Typed	Appears	Means
123	1.23E+02	$1.23*100$ or $1.23*10^2$
.0123	1.23E-02	$1.23*.01$ or $1.23/100$
4563452.7	4.56E+06	$4.56*1,000,000$ or $4.56*10^6$

- **Leading Zeros** format puts sufficient zeros in front of a number so that a specified number of significant figures show to the left of the decimal point.

- **True/False** format displays the word *TRUE* or *FALSE* in the cell in accordance with the truth of the statement in the cell. For example, the statement *C3>5* will display *TRUE* if the value in C3 is greater than 5 and *FALSE* if it is equal or less.

- **Calculations** are always done with the entire number, regardless of how many significant figures are currently displayed in a cell. Calculations are done with eight figures of precision.

ACTIVITY 8.11

Formatting Numbers in a Spreadsheet

1. Be sure that MYCITY.WKS (or MYCITYFO.WKS) is the active spreadsheet.

2. Select a range and apply the Fixed number format.

   select the range D5:D12

   choose Format, Number

   click the Fixed option

   *type **1** in the* Number of decimals *text box and click OK*

3. Select a range and apply a Comma format.

   select the range E5:F12

choose Format, Number

click the Comma option

type **0** *in the* Number of decimals *box and click OK*

ACTIVITY 8.12
Adding a Border

1. Add lines at the bottom of the columns.

    select the range D10:E10

    choose Format, Border

    click the Bottom border

    choose a thin line style (second from the top)

    click OK

2. Add a border.

    select the range C12:E12

    choose Format, Border

    choose Outline

    click OK

3. Save, print, and close the spreadsheet.

Using the Format Icons

You can use the format icons in the Toolbar to do limited number formatting. These apply the currency, percentage, and comma formats to a selected range. The format uses the default two significant figures to the right of the decimal.

On Your Own

Format the MYLABOR.WKS spreadsheet or, if you didn't do the case study, the LABORF.WKS spreadsheet.

1. Open the MYLABOR.WKS (or LABORF.WKS) spreadsheet.

2.   Apply the following formats.

Select the title *Labor Rates* and give it a size and style of 14 point bold (type the size in the *Font* box).

Widen column E so the label *Overhead* is not truncated.

Center the labels in the range B3:G4 using the Center icon.

Center column A and the label in G13.

Format the range C6:G9 and cell G11 with the Currency format. Use the icon.

Format the range G14:G16 with a Percentage format with 0 decimal places.

3.   Save, print, and close the spreadsheet.

Dates and Times

You learned in the last chapter that Works stores dates as consecutive whole numbers and times as fractional numbers. The appearance of the date or time is determined by the format. If you type in the date or time in a form that Works recognizes, it will automatically be formatted as a date or time. If you later choose a numeric format, the date or time will appear as a number.

Some of the date and time forms that the spreadsheet program recognizes:

7/23/92   or   July 23, 1992

10/4   or   Oct 4   (Works assumes you mean the current year)

14:30   or   2:30 PM

After a date or time has been entered you may change its format with the Format, Number command. Works gives a number of date formats in the *Number* dialog box. You can also create a series of dates with the Edit, Fill Series command. In the next activity you will determine how old you are using dates.

ACTIVITY 8.13

Entering and Formatting Dates and Times

1. Create a spreadsheet.

2. Enter two dates.

   in cell B2, enter today's date in an M/D/Y format (for example, 7/16/93)

   in cell B3, enter your birthday in an M/D/Y format

3. Find your age.

   in cell B4 type **=B2-B3** *to find your age in days*

   format cell B4 with a Fixed format and 0 significant figures

4. Format a time.

   type **.5** *in cell D5*

   choose Format, Number

   click the Time option button

   select the top format in the Time *list box*

   click OK

   Works formats the time as 12:00 PM, one-half day since midnight.

5. Close the spreadsheet without saving the changes.

Case Study

In this case study you will use what you have learned to construct a checkbook spreadsheet.

1. Create a spreadsheet.

2. In cell B1 type **1994 CHECKING ACCOUNT** and format it as bold.

3. In cell D3 type **Beginning Balance** and in cell G3 enter **613.63**. Format the value as currency with two decimal points.

4. Add the following headings:

Cell	Heading
A5	**Rtn.**
B5	**Ck#**
C5	**Date**
D5	**Item**
E5	**Debit**
F5	**Credit**
G5	**Balance**
H5	**Comments**

5. In rows 6 through 10 add the following text and numbers to columns A through F.

	A	B	C	D	E	F
5						
6	*		1/1/94	Beginning Balance	0	0
7	*		1/2/94	Deposit	0	4068.75
8	*	242	1/2/94	Master Card	2189.89	0
9	*	244	1/2/94	Rent	700	0
10	*		1/2/94	Most	100	0
11						

6. In cell G6 enter a formula that will place a copy of the Beginning Balance in cell G6.

7. In cell G7 enter a formula that will subtract the contents of cell E7 and add the contents of cell F7 to G6. The balance in G7 equals the balance in the cell above plus any credit in row 7 minus any debit in row 7.

8. Fill the formula in G7 into the range G8:G10.

9. Format columns E, F, and G as currency with two decimal points.

10. Type the word **Computer** in cell H8.

11. Insert a row between present rows 8 and 9.

12. Type the entries *****, **243, 1/2/94, Doctor, 200.43, 0** in the range A9:F9.

13. Copy the Balance formula down into cell G10.

14. Add the entries ***, , 1/3/94, Deposit, 0, 288.00** to the bottom row of the checkbook.

Spreadsheet

15. Copy the formula in column G into the new row.

16. In cells E15 and F15 use the Sum icon to total the Debits and Credits column.

17. Make any corrections and additions necessary. Make all formats consistent. Save the worksheet as CHKBOOK.WKS. Close the worksheet.

Quick Check

1. What are two ways to align cell entries?

2. What is a disadvantage of formatting a number as right- or center-aligned?

3. How would you format a number as $5,342,543?

4. What is the difference between "relative" and "absolute" copying?

5. How do you insert a row? What happens to the row above? below?

6. What are two ways of changing a column width?

7. Name the nine number formats.

Functions and Features

9

Overview

In an earlier chapter you used a few simple functions to find the sum and average of a column of numbers. In this chapter you'll be introduced to advanced functions that will do calculations you might not be able to do any other way. You will also be shown special features of the spreadsheet program that help you display and protect your data. Finally, you will be introduced to larger spreadsheets and learn how to easily move through them.

Objectives

- Understand the use of functions and arguments
- Create a monthly payment table for various terms
- Learn about range names
- Sort rows in a spreadsheet
- Protect parts of your spreadsheet
- Freeze parts of the spreadsheet while you scroll through the rest
- Divide your spreadsheet into panes

Function Basics

A **function** is a special type of spreadsheet formula, consisting of a name and one or more arguments. The syntax (grammar) of the function consists of the equal sign, a function name, and arguments in parentheses.

The **Function name** tells Works what you want done with the data furnished in the arguments.

The **Arguments** are enclosed within parentheses following the name of the function and supply the information that the function needs. If more than one argument is supplied, the arguments are separated by commas. Some functions take no arguments (but still require the parentheses).

Some examples of ways functions can be used:

=SUM(A3:A23)	Finds the sum of the values in the range A3:A23. The name of the function is **SUM** and the single argument is the range A3:A23.
=SUM(3,4,5,6)	Finds the sum of 3+4+5+6. This time there are four arguments to the SUM function.
=SUM(inventory)	Finds the sum of the values in a range named *inventory*. The single argument is the name of the range.
=PMT(8000,7%/12,48)	Finds the monthly payment for an $8,000 loan at 7 percent for 48 months. The function name is **PMT**. The three arguments are the loan amount, the periodic loan rate, and the number of periods. Arguments must be entered in the correct order.

Your *User's Guide to Microsoft Works* lists more than 50 functions with their arguments and examples of how they can be used. You can also use Help for quick list of functions and arguments.

Entering Functions

Just as with a formula, there is more than one way to enter a function into a spreadsheet. The techniques are similar. In the next activity you will practice the various methods with the SUM() function.

ACTIVITY 9.1
Entering Arguments into a Function

1. Create a spreadsheet.

2. Add some data.

   use the data shown here

	A	B	C
1			
2		2	
3		5	
4		1	
5		8	
6		5	
7		6	
8			

3. Sum the data.

   in cell B9 type **=SUM(B2:B7)** *and press* ⏎**ENTER**

4. Clear the cell and try another method.

   clear cell B9

   in cell B9 type **=SUM(**

   use the mouse to drag through the range B2:B7 and note the result in the Formula bar and in the active cell

   type the closing **)** *and press* ⏎**ENTER**

5. Clear the cell and use the keyboard.

   clear cell B9

   in cell B9 type **=SUM(**

   use the arrow keys to move to cell B7

   hold down **SHIFT** *and use* ↑ *to extend the selection through the range B2:B7*

   type the closing **)** *and release* **SHIFT** *, then press* ⏎**ENTER**

6. If you're continuing on to the next activity, leave this spreadsheet open. Otherwise, close the spreadsheet and do not save the changes.

Other Types of Functions

You can duplicate the results from the SUM() function using simple addition, although this is difficult if the column of numbers is lengthy. Other functions perform mathematical calculations that are more difficult and for which we frequently don't know the equations. Such a function is the PMT() function, which calculates a monthly (or any periodic) payment if you know the amount borrowed, the interest rate, and the number of periods in the term of the loan.

When you use the payment function, you must enter the interest rate in terms of the length of a period. For example, if you are calculating a monthly payment, then the interest rate must be the monthly rate (the yearly rate divided by 12), and the number of periods must be the number of months.

A loan of $10,000 with a 7 percent yearly interest rate for 4 years would use the following arguments:

Principal	10000	don't use a $ or commas
Rate	.07/12	use a monthly interest rate—0.07 or 7%
Term	48	number of months in the term

Thus the function would appear as **=PMT(10000,.07/12,48)**. The arguments must be in the proper order and be separated from one another by commas.

You can also use cell references as arguments to the function. This would be a better way to do a "what-if" analysis of the effect on the monthly payment of changes in one of the arguments. Put the arguments in input cells where they are easy to change.

ACTIVITY 9.2

The Payment Function

1. Clear the spreadsheet or create a new one.

2. Enter the function.

    in cell F4 type the function **=PMT(10000,.07/12,48)**

    The function returns (displays the value calculated by the function) a value for the monthly payment of 239.46.

3. Use input cells for the arguments.

    type headings of **Principal**, **Rate**, **No. Months**, *and* **Monthly Pmt.** *in cells B3, C3, D3, and F3, respectively*

    enter values of **10000**, **7**, *and* **48** *in cells B4, C4, and D4, respectively*

    retype the function in F4 to read **=PMT(B4,C4/1200,D4)**

    By using *C4/1200* as an argument, you will first convert the rate to a percent and then to a monthly rate. The monthly payment should still be 239.46.

    try other values for the principal, rate, and term

4. Close the file without saving *unless* you are going to do the On Your Own that follows.

On Your Own

Construct a table of monthly payments for different terms. Use the spreadsheet you were working on in the last activity.

1. In cell D4 type the number 6. Select the range D4:D13, then choose Edit, Fill Series with a Step By of 6.

2. Select the range F4:F13 and fill the function in F4 into the other cells.

3. If you get an obviously incorrect result, check the arguments to the functions in cells F5:B13. Do you need to use absolute references for some of the arguments?

4. Are there interesting facts to be learned from the table? Is the monthly payment for the 30-month term twice the payment for the 60-month term? Could you use the table to figure out the best set of payments for your budget? This is a simple, but useful, example of "what-if" analysis.

5. Build a similar table, but this time let the rate vary instead of the term.

6. Add a column to one of the previous tables that shows the interest paid for the different rates or terms. Hint: The total interest is the monthly payment times the number of periods minus the principal borrowed.

7. In another part of the spreadsheet make a table of the numbers between 1 and 20 and their square roots. Look up the appropriate function in Help.

Named Ranges and Manual Recalculation

Named Ranges—You can select a range and give it a name, then use the name as a function argument or with the Go To command. To name a range, select the range first, then choose Edit, Range Name. To use the range, enter the name of the range as a function argument or choose the Edit, Go To command.

Manual Calculation and Recalculate Now—If you have a very large spreadsheet or a very slow computer, you may find that each time you enter a value involved in a calculation there is a considerable pause as the spreadsheet is recalculated. This can become annoying if you're in a hurry. To override the automatic recalculation, choose Tools, Manual Calculation. Then when you have finished entering data, choose Tools, Calculate Now, or press [F9], to have all the calculations redone. *Don't forget to recalculate!*

In the next activity you will use Insert, Range Name, Calculate Now, and the RAND() and INT() functions. RAND() is a function that requires no arguments and returns a random decimal fraction between 0 and 1. Each time you do something that causes the spreadsheet to recalculate, the value returned by RAND() changes. The INT() function returns the integer (whole) part of a decimal number. For example, the integer part of the 234.67811 is 234. INT() does not round up a number to the next integer.

You can also use functions together. For example, suppose the RAND() function returns the value 0.23467811. Then =100*RAND() would have returned 23.467811. Combining this with the INT() function you could write =INT(100*RAND()) and expect the value 23, the integer portion of 23.467811. Works will first calculate the RAND() function because it inside the parentheses of the INT() function. The value returned by the function will be multiplied by 100. The INT() function will then return the integer part of the product. Note that you must have as many left parentheses as right parentheses. The formula can return any integer between 0 and 99. To have it return any integer between 1 and 100, make it read =INT(100*RAND())+1.

ACTIVITY 9.3

Using Range Names, Recalculation, and Some New Functions

1. Create a spreadsheet.

2. Turn off automatic recalculation.

    choose Tools, Manual Calculation

    A check mark is placed beside the command.

3. Enter the formula to calculate a random number between 1 and 100.

    type the formula **=INT(100*RAND())+1** *in cell A3 and press* [ENTER]

    What number did you get? Each time you use the formula, you should get a different random number.

4. Fill a range with the formula. In the next steps, do not click in the spreadsheet to deselect the range.

    select the range A3:E22, consisting of 100 cells

    choose Edit, Fill Right and then choose Edit, Fill Down

Why does this work?

5.   Name the range.

with the range still selected, choose Insert, Range Name

type **RANDOM** *in the* Name *text box and click OK*

6.   Find the sum and average of the values in the range.

in cell A1 type **AVG**, *in cell B1 type* **MAX**, *and in cell C1 type* **MIN**

in cell A2 type the function and argument **=AVG(RANDOM)**

in cell B2 type the function and argument **=MAX(RANDOM)**

in cell C2 type the function and argument **=MIN(RANDOM)**

7.   Recalculate the spreadsheet with a new set of values.

choose Tools, Calculate Now, or press F9

8.   Save the spreadsheet with the name RANDOM.WKS and close it.

The IF() function

There may be occasions where the results displayed in your spreadsheet should depend on a value calculated somewhere else. For example you might want the amount of a discount applied to an order to depend on the size of the order.

You can use the IF() function to have Works make decisions for you. The IF() function takes three arguments:

1.   A comparison. For example, are the contents of cell B3 larger than 100?

2.   If the answer is true, the function displays the results of the second argument.

3.   If the answer is false, the function displays the results of the third argument.

Spreadsheet

Comparisons are made using the logical operators =, >, < , >=, <= , and <>.

Operator	Meaning
A=B	if A equals B
A>B	if A is greater than B
A<B	if A is less than B
A>=B	if A is greater than or equal to B
A<=B	if A is less than or equal to B
A<>B	if A is not equal to B

ACTIVITY 9.4

Using the IF() function

1. Create a spreadsheet and enter the data from the figure below.

	A	B	C	D
1	Company	Order	After Discount	
2				
3	Johnson's	300		
4	BMart	175		
5	ReddiShop	250		
6				

2. Use the IF() function to calculate a discount.

    in C3 type the function =IF(B3>=250, B3*.85, B3)

    The function says: If B3 is greater than or equal to 250, then return the value of B3 multiplied by 0.85; otherwise, return just the value of B3.

    drag through the range C3:C5

    choose Edit, Fill Down to enter the function into the remaining cells

    format the range as Currency

Only the companies that have bought $250 or more are eligible for a 15 percent discount (.85 = 1.00 - .15). Johnson's pays $255, ReddiShop $212.50, and BMart pays the full amount.

3. Leave the spreadsheet open for the next activity.

Formatting with True and False

If you place a statement that makes a comparison within a cell in the spreadsheet program, the result will be true or false. For example, if you type =3>4, the result is false, since 3 is not greater than 4. Works responds by placing a 0 in the cell if the statement is false and a 1 if the statement is true. If you format the cell the cell as True/False, the word *TRUE* or *FALSE* will appear.

ACTIVITY 9.5

True and False Statements

1. Type a True/False statement.

   type =3>4 in cell B9 and press ⌈ENTER⌉

   A 0 appears to show that the statement is false.

2. Format the cell.

   choose Format, Number, True/False

   The word *FALSE* appears in the cell.

3. Reverse the 3 and the 4 and view the results.

4. Close the spreadsheet and do not save the changes.

Sorting the Rows in a Spreadsheet Range

After you have added data to a spreadsheet you may want to sort the rows so that items will appear in alphabetic or numeric order as you read down a column. However, the column that you want sorted may be keyed to data in adjacent columns that you want to stay beside the data in the sorted column.

	A	B	C
1	FIRST NAME	LAST NAME	OWED
2	Lucille	Barker	$14.59
3	Betty	Martinez	$40.22
4	Terry	Randolph	$16.84
5	Gene	Smith	$84.11
6	Aaron	Smith	$17.54

To be sure the data in a row remains together during a sort, select the data before sorting (don't include the heading or it will be sorted, too). In the example select A2:C6. Then choose Tools, Sort Rows. Type the number of the column containing the sort key in the *1st Column* box. In the example, to sort on the LAST NAME, type **B** in the box and click OK. You will find the rows are sorted on the basis of the last names in column B, but the first names may still not be in alphabetical order for the people with the same last name. To sort based on last name and first name within identical last names, type **B** in the *1st Column* box and **A** in the *2nd Column* box.

You can sort in ascending or descending order, depending on the option chosen below the appropriate column text box. Ascending means that sorting will start with A or 1 at the top of the column and go to Z or the highest number at the bottom of the column.

ACTIVITY 9.6

Sorting on Rows

1. Open the spreadsheet MYCITY.WKS (or MYCITYFO.WKS) from the student diskette.

2. Sort the cities.

    select the range B5:F10

    choose Tools, Sort Rows

    *type **B** in the* 1st Column *box and click OK*

    The data is sorted on the basis of the names of the cities. Can you sort it back into the original order? Should you have included the serial numbers in column A in the sort?

3. Close the spreadsheet without saving the changes.

4. Reopen the spreadsheet and do the sort again, this time including column A.

    select the range A5:E10

    choose Tools, Sort Rows

    *type **B** in the* 1st Column *box and click OK*

5. Sort the spreadsheet back into its original order.

    select the range A5:F10

choose Tools, Sort Rows

type **A** *in the* 1st Column *box and click OK*

6. Close the spreadsheet and do not save the changes.

On Your Own

1. Open the LABOR.WKS or LABORF.WKS spreadsheet from the student diskette.

2. Sort the labor cost spreadsheet based on the last names, first in ascending and then descending order.

Protecting a Spreadsheet

If you create a spreadsheet that will be used by others, you may want to protect certain areas against inadvertent changes, while leaving other ranges free for data entry. You can lock a cell or range to prevent changes from being made. You can unlock it later.

When you open a new spreadsheet, every cell is locked. However, the protection for the entire spreadsheet has been turned off. You might think of it as having an electric fence around each cell with the electricity off. Because the protection is turned off, you can enter data in any cell.

You may unlock a cell while the protection is turned off. Then, when you turn the protection on, every cell will be locked except those you had previously unlocked. Now you can enter data only in the unlocked cells. In a like manner, you relock a cell by turning the protection off, locking the cell, and then turning the protection back on.

To lock or unlock a range of cells, choose Format, Protection, then mark or clear the Locked check box. To turn on spreadsheet protection, mark the Protect Data check box.

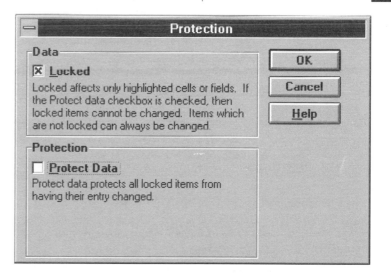

ACTIVITY 9.7

Unlocking a Range

1. Open the LABORF.WKS spreadsheet. All cells are locked, but the protection is turned off.

2. Unlock a range.

    select the range G14:G16

    choose Format, Protection and clear the Locked check box

3. Protect the spreadsheet.

    mark the Protect Data check box

    At this point you have unlocked a range of cells and protected the spreadsheet. While the spreadsheet is protected, you will be able to enter data only into the unlocked range.

4. Test the protection.

    change the overhead rate in the unlocked cell G15 to **1.2**

    The data can be entered and the spreadsheet recalculated.

    change the direct labor rate for John Smith in cell C6 to **7.15**

    Works responds with a message that the cell is locked.

5. Remove the protection and change the value.

    choose Format, Protection and clear the Protect Data check box

    change the direct labor rate for John Smith in cell C6 to **7.15**

6. Close the spreadsheet without saving the changes.

On Your Own

1. Open the LABOR.WKS spreadsheet from the student diskette.

2. Unlock the range containing the direct labor rates.

3. Protect the document so only the rates can be changed.

4. Check to see if only the direct labor rates can be changed.

5. Close the document and do not save the changes.

Navigating Larger Spreadsheets

Most of the work you have done so far has been confined to a single screen. In a larger spreadsheet, you need methods of moving quickly to various areas. Works provides a number of ways to do this.

With the Mouse

Use the scroll bars to move to a new location. *Using the scroll bars does not change the location of the active cell.*

- Clicking the arrows at the end of the vertical scroll bar moves your view up or down one line.

- Clicking the arrows at the end of the horizontal scroll bar moves your view left or right one column.

- Clicking above or below the vertical scroll box moves your view up or down one window.

- Clicking right or left of the horizontal scroll box moves your view right or left one window.

- Dragging the scroll box moves your view in the spreadsheet to a position approximately proportional to the position of the box within the scroll bar.

- When you use the scroll bars to move to a new viewing location in your spreadsheet, the active range does not change. Click a cell within the new window to place the active cell somewhere in the viewing area.

Spreadsheet

With the Keyboard

Key/Combination	Action
[Left Arrow], [Right Arrow], [Up Arrow], or [Down Arrow]	moves one column or row in the direction of the key arrow
[Home]	moves to the beginning of a row
[End]	moves to the last cell in the row
[Page Up]	moves up one window
[Page Down]	moves down one window
[Ctrl] [Home]	moves to the beginning of the spreadsheet
[Ctrl] [End]	moves to the end of the active spreadsheet
[Ctrl] [Page Up]	moves one window to the left
[Ctrl] [Page Down]	moves one window to the right
[Ctrl] [Arrow Key]	moves to the end of the data block in the direction of the arrow
[F5]	go to a specified cell or range name

In the next activity you will open a larger spreadsheet and practice moving around.

ACTIVITY 9.8

Moving in a Larger Spreadsheet

1. Open the INVEST.WKS spreadsheet from the student diskette.

2. Move around in the spreadsheet.

   press **[CTRL] [HOME]** *to go to the beginning of the spreadsheet*

   press **[↓]** *5 times to go to row 6*

   press **[END]** *to go to the right edge of the active spreadsheet*

   press **[CTRL] [PG↑]** *to move left one window*

press **F5** *and type* **D6** *in the* Go To *text box and click OK*

press **CTRL** **↓** *repeatedly, moving from block to block until you reach cell D54*

If you go too far you'll find yourself at the bottom of the spreadsheet. Press [Ctrl] [Up] to move up to the first block.

press **CTRL** **→** *3 times to move horizontally from one data block to the next*

3. Experiment with the scroll bars.

    click to the left of the scroll box in the horizontal scroll bar

    click above the scroll box in the vertical scroll bar

    drag the scroll box to the right end of the horizontal scroll bar

    Note that the active cell is not in the window.

4. Experiment with other keyboard commands to move around the spreadsheet.

Freezing Titles

Many times in a large spreadsheet, the titles you need to see have scrolled off the window by the time you get to the data you want to work with. When this happens, it may be difficult to know whether you are in the correct row or column. To help with this problem, Works lets you freeze columns, rows, or both, while scrolling through the rest of the spreadsheet. A column or columns containing titles will stay fixed while you scroll horizontally through the rest of the spreadsheet, and a row of titles will remain fixed as you scroll vertically. If you like, you may have both horizontal and vertical titles remain fixed. To freeze titles, move the active cell to the desired location and use the Format, Freeze Titles command. To freeze:

*   **Horizontally**—Move the active cell into column A and the row below where you want the titles frozen. Choose Format, Freeze Titles.

*   **Vertically**—Move the active cell into row 1 and the column to the right of where you want the titles frozen. Choose Format, Freeze Titles.

- **Both**—Move the active cell into the row below and the column to the right of where the titles are to be frozen. Choose Format, Freeze Titles.

- To **thaw** the titles, choose Format, Freeze Titles again to remove the check mark from the command.

	A	H	I	J
3		1993	Feb 93	
4			SHARES	PRICE	VALUE
13	Kemper High-Yield Fund	3553	7.84	$27,853
14	Kemper Money Market Portfolio	15955	1.00	$15,955
15	Kemper US Govt. Securities	3996	9.05	$36,167
16	Liberty US Govt Money Market Trust	8309	1.00	$8,309
17	TransAmerica Govt. Sec. Trust (Crit.)	5831	8.06	$46,996
18	Van Kampen Merritt US Govt Fd	212	15.32	$3,245
19	SubTotal			$289,696
20				

ACTIVITY 9.9

Freezing a Vertical Column of Titles

1. Make INVEST.WKS the active spreadsheet.

2. Move to the upper left corner of the spreadsheet.

   press **CTRL** **HOME**

3. Freeze column A.

   press **→** *to move to cell B1*

   choose Format, Freeze Titles

   press **CTRL** **PG↓**

   The window scrolls to the right but the titles in column A stay fixed.

   choose Format, Freeze Titles to thaw the titles

4. Freeze rows 3 and 4.

   press **↓** *until rows 1 and 2 scroll off the top of the screen*

   click cell A5

choose Format, Freeze Titles to freeze the titles in rows 3 and 4

press **[PG↓]**

The window scrolls down but the titles in rows 3 and 4 stay fixed at the top of the window.

choose Format, Freeze Titles to thaw the titles

5. Freeze both vertical and horizontal titles.

press **[↓]** *until rows 1 and 2 scroll off the top of the screen*

click cell B5

choose Format, Freeze Titles to freeze the titles

choose View, Gridlines to hide the grid lines

Works displays solid lines to indicate where the spreadsheet is frozen.

move around in the spreadsheet to check that both horizontal and vertical titles stay fixed

choose Format, Freeze Titles to thaw the titles

choose View, Gridlines to show the grid lines

6. Leave the spreadsheet open for the next activity.

Splitting the Spreadsheet into Panes

Splitting a spreadsheet and freezing titles are somewhat alike, but splitting means you can have more than one window looking on the same spreadsheet. For example, perhaps you would like to see the December 92 column displayed next to the December 93 column even though they are several windows apart. By choosing the Window, Split command you can divide the window into separate panes, with each displaying a copy of the spreadsheet together with scroll bars so you can scroll through each pane independently.

As shown in the figure below, when you choose the Window, Split command the mouse pointer becomes a four-headed arrow. Attached to the arrows are horizontal and vertical bars that you can move to the position where you want the spreadsheet split into panes. Click when the bars are in the correct location. If you want just two panes, move the extra bar into the labels at the top or left edge of the spreadsheet.

Spreadsheet

	A	B	C	D	E	F	
				INVEST.WKS			
1		)SR Investment Program					
2							
3	1993	Dec 92			Jan 93		
4		SHARES	PRICE	VALUE	SHARES	PRICE	V
5	MUTUAL FUNDS						
6	AARP Capital Growth Fund	346	29.82	$10,318	346	30.23	$
7	AARP GNMA & US Treasury	2592	15.56	$40,327	2592	15.72	$
8	AARP Growth and Income Fund	1526	26.67	$40,686	1526	26.97	$
9	AARP High Quality Money Fund	5016	1.00	$5,016	5039	1.00	
10	AARP High Quality Bond Fund	1308	15.44	$20,200	1316	15.71	$
11	Colonial Income Trust Fund Inc	302	5.97	$1,803	305	5.96	
12	Dreyfus Inter Tax Ex Bond Fund	2434	13.48	$32,810	2444	13.54	$
13	Kemper High-Yield Fund	3451	7.01	$24,194	3506	7.13	$
14	Kemper Money Market Portfolio	24022	1.00	$24,022	15848	1.00	$

ACTIVITY 9.10

Dividing a Spreadsheet into Panes

1. Make INVEST.WKS the active spreadsheet.

2. Split the spreadsheet vertically into two panes. Don't click until you have the horizontal and vertical bars in position.

   choose Window, Split

   move the vertical bar in between columns D and E

   move the horizontal bar up into the row of column labels

   click

3. Review the December 92 and 93 results alongside each other.

   click in the right pane

   use the horizontal scroll bar to scroll through the right pane until the December 93 results are displayed next to the December 92 results

   drag the bar separating the two panes to adjust your view

	A	B	C	D	E
1		DSR Investment Program			
2					
3	1993		Dec 92		
4		SHARES	PRICE	VALUE	SHARES
5	MUTUAL FUNDS				
6	AARP Capital Growth Fund	346	29.82	$10,318	346
7	AARP GNMA & US Treasury	2592	15.56	$40,327	2592
8	AARP Growth and Income Fund	1526	26.67	$40,686	1526
9	AARP High Quality Money Fund	5016	1.00	$5,016	5039
10	AARP High Quality Bond Fund	1308	15.44	$20,200	1316
11	Colonial Income Trust Fund Inc	302	5.97	$1,803	305
12	Dreyfus Inter Tax Ex Bond Fund	2434	13.48	$32,810	2444
13	Kemper High-Yield Fund	3451	7.01	$24,194	3506
14	Kemper Money Market Portfolio	24022	1.00	$24,022	15848

4. Remove the split.

   drag the bar separating the two panes into the row labels

5. Close the spreadsheet without saving the changes.

	A	B	C	D	AL	AM	AN
3	1993		Dec 92			Dec 93	
4		SHARES	PRICE	VALUE	SHARES	PRICE	VALUE
5	MUTUAL FUNDS						
6	AARP Capital Growth Fund	346	29.82	$10,318	359	31.94	$11,461
7	AARP GNMA & US Treasury	2592	15.56	$40,327	2592	16.13	$41,804
8	AARP Growth and Income Fund	1526	26.67	$40,686	1577	28.08	$44,270
9	AARP High Quality Money Fund	5016	1.00	$5,016	5111	1.00	$5,111
10	AARP High Quality Bond Fund	1308	15.44	$20,200	1337	16.29	$21,774
11	Colonial Income Trust Fund Inc	302	5.97	$1,803	334	6.47	$2,163
12	Dreyfus Inter Tax Ex Bond Fund	2434	13.48	$32,810	2187	13.95	$30,515
13	Kemper High-Yield Fund	3451	7.01	$24,194	3010	8.95	$34,098
14	Kemper Money Market Portfolio	24022	1.00	$24,022	2351	1.00	$2,351
15	Kemper US Govt. Securities	3935	9.02	$35,497	4028	9.65	$38,866
16	Liberty US Govt Money Market	8309	1.00	$8,309	8335	1.00	$8,335
17	TransAmerica Govt. Sec. Trust	5831	0.07	$47,054	5831	8.52	$49,678
18	Van Kampen Merritt US Govt Fd	212	15.25	$3,231	232	16.13	$3,741
19	SubTotal			$293,468			$294,168
20							
21	BONDS						
22	St. Francis Medical Cntr. 9%			$5,000			$5,000

Quick Check

1. What is an argument? What is the syntax (grammar) of a function?

2. What would your monthly payments be if you bought a car costing $18,000 and took a 5-year loan at 15.9 percent? How much interest would you pay?

Spreadsheet

3. What are some possible ways of entering ranges as arguments to a function?

4. What shortcut keys move to the beginning of a spreadsheet? the end?

5. How can you ensure that a cell's contents are not changed accidentally?

6. What are the steps in sorting the rows in a spreadsheet?

7. What are the steps if you want to freeze rows 3 and 4 at the top of the spreadsheet while you scroll down?

8. Why might you want to turn off automatic recalculation? If you turn on manual recalculation, what must you remember to do?

Charting

10

Overview

A chart or graph is one of the best ways of portraying data in an easily understood form. If data represents trees, then a chart is a view of the forest. With Works, data in a worksheet can be converted to one of six chart types. Each can then be further refined with custom formatting to provide titles, a legend, and colors and patterns. The chart is automatically updated as the spreadsheet data changes. You will also take another look at printing spreadsheets and charts in this chapter.

Objectives

- Enter data for charting
- Select data and create a chart
- Understand the parts of a chart
- Change colors and patterns in a chart
- Edit a chart
- Print charts
- Add page breaks and print larger spreadsheets

Works Charts

Creating a chart in Works involves selecting the data and then telling Works what type of chart to build. The selected data should include both the numeric data that is to be plotted and the names of the data categories. For example, the chart on the next page was created by selecting the range B2:D6, then clicking the Chart icon on the Toolbar. The Chart icon has a small bar chart with a bubbling test tube on its face and is to the right of the Sum icon. After you make some choices in the *New Chart* dialog box, Works will create the chart in a window of its own.

Spreadsheet

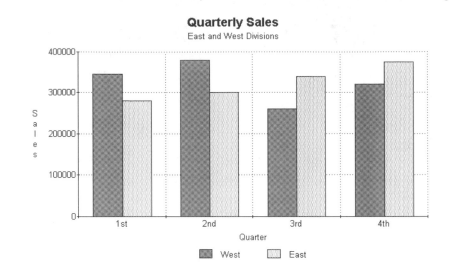

After the chart has been created you can choose from the 12 chart types. The data selection includes the data in the range C3:D6, the category headings in column B3:B6, and the legend in row C2:D2.

Parts of a Chart

As you learn how to create and format charts, you will need to know the names of the components of a chart. Use the figure below as a guide to the names and functions of various chart parts.

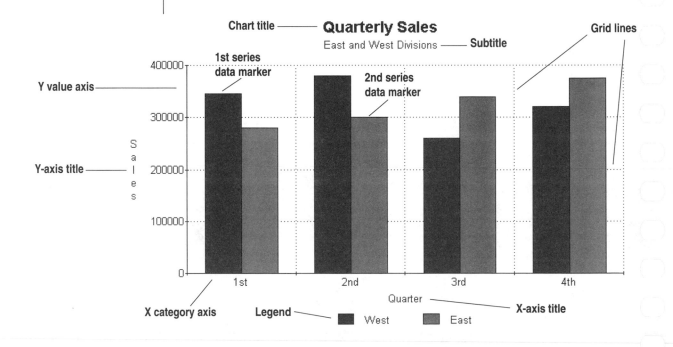

Chart—The entire area inside the chart window.

Data Marker—A data marker is a column, dot, or other symbol that marks a data point. The position of the point or height of the column is related to the magnitude of the value it represents and its position within a data series.

Data Series—The series of related data points. The four left-hand columns form the West data series.

Axis—A horizontal or vertical line that marks the bottom or left side of the plotted area. The horizontal line at the base of the chart is called the X or Category axis, and the vertical line is called the Y or Value axis. The magnitude of the data is shown numerically along the Y-axis.

Gridlines—Dotted lines that extend the markings on the Value and Category axes.

Title—The name you give the chart. You can also give names to the X and Y axes.

Legend—A key that identifies and names the data series.

Creating a Chart

When you create a chart, it appears in its own window with a different menu and icons. You can move between the chart and data windows with the Window command.

In the next activity you will create a chart using the data shown here.

	C	D	E
2			
3		West	East
4	1st	345000	280000
5	2nd	380000	300000
6	3rd	260000	340000
7	4th	320000	375000
8			

ACTIVITY 10.1

Prepare the Data and Create a Chart

1. Create a spreadsheet.

2. Enter the data.

   type the data as shown in the above example into the cells

3. Select the data and create the chart.

   select the range C3:E7

   click the Chart icon or choose Tools, Create New Chart

4. Make the desired selections in the dialog box.

click the arrow in the What type of chart do you want? *box and note the chart types*

choose Bar

type **Quarterly Sales** *in the* Chart title *box*

mark the three option buttons as shown in the example above

If you like, you can see the effects of the other choices.

click OK when your choices look like the example

5. Save the spreadsheet.

choose Window and click the name of the spreadsheet (Sheet1)

choose File, Save As and save the spreadsheet and chart with the name MYDATA.WKS

NOTE: When you save a spreadsheet, you also save all the charts associated with it. When you close a spreadsheet, you close the charts as well.

Chart Types

There are 12 chart types and each one can be formatted in four to six ways. The type and format that is best depends on your taste and the chart data.

Area chart—The area under the data markers is filled with a solid pattern.

Bar chart—Each value in the data series is represented by a vertical bar (column). The bar chart is the default type.

Line chart—The data markers are points that are usually connected by straight lines in the chart.

Pie chart—A circular chart divided in proportion to the relative magnitude of the values in a data series. A pie chart can show only a single data series.

Stacked line—Like a line chart, except the lines represent the sums of the data series.

X-Y or scatter chart—Shows the relationship between two data series by positioning markers along both the horizontal and vertical axes.

Radar chart Data is plotted in radial fashion around a central point.

Combination chart—A combination of two chart types such as bar and line.

3-D area chart—The area chart is shown in a three dimensional view.

3-D bar chart—The bar chart is shown in a three-dimensional view.

3-D line chart—The line chart is shown in a three-dimensional view.

3-D pie chart—The pie chart is shown in a three-dimensional view.

To choose a chart type, click the corresponding icon, or choose Gallery and select from the list of commands. When you choose a chart type, you are given several formats to choose from. Select the one that comes closest to the format you want.

Spreadsheet

ACTIVITY 10.2

Looking at Chart Types

1. Make MYDATA.WKS the active spreadsheet.

2. Choose the chart.

    choose Window and click Chart1

3. Choose a chart type.

    click the Line Chart icon or choose Gallery, Line

    in the Line *dialog box click format 5*

    click OK for a line chart with X and Y gridlines

4. Repeat the steps above, choosing each of the other chart types. The X-Y (scatter) chart requires a different type of data.

5. Return to the original chart type.

    click the Bar icon

    select format 1 in the Bar *dialog box and click OK*

6. Save and leave the spreadsheet open for the next activity.

Naming and Saving, Duplicating, and Deleting Charts

You can have several charts associated with a single spreadsheet. Different charts may use different sets of data within the spreadsheet, or they may use the same data but be of different chart types. To begin with, each chart is given the name ChartX where X is a number assigned by Works.

*   To name a chart choose Tools, Name Chart. In the *Name Chart* dialog box select the name (ChartX) that you want to rename from the *Charts* list box. Type the new name in the *Name* text box. Click the Rename button and the OK button.

*   To duplicate a chart, choose Tools, Duplicate Chart. In the *Duplicate Chart* dialog box, select the name of the chart that you want to duplicate, then type a new name in the *Name* text box. Click the Duplicate and OK buttons.

*   To delete a chart, Choose Tools, Delete Chart. In the *Delete Chart* dialog box select the chart you want to delete and click the Delete and OK buttons.

elf

- To save the charts in the charts list, save the associated spreadsheet. The charts automatically save with the spreadsheet.

- You will find the Tools commands in both the spreadsheet and the chart windows.

ACTIVITY 10.3

Naming and Duplicating a Chart

1. Name the chart you created.

    choose Tools, Name Chart

    select Chart1 *in the* Charts *list box*

    type **Bar 1** *in the* Name *text box*

    click the Rename button

    click OK

2. Duplicate a chart and give it a different format.

    choose Tools, Duplicate Chart

    select Bar 1 *in the* Charts *list box*

    type the new name **Line 1** *in the* Name *text box*

    click Duplicate and then click OK

    choose View, Charts and click Line 1

    click the Line icon and select format 4 in the Line *dialog box*

    click OK

3. Use the same methods to create a pie chart and name it *PIE 1* (only the first data series will be used for the chart). Use chart format 5.

4. Delete a chart.

    choose Tools, Delete Chart

    select Line 1

    click Delete and then click OK to leave the dialog box

5. Save and close your spreadsheet.

Spreadsheet

How Data Selection Affects a Chart

The way in which you select a chart range will affect the way a chart appears. Works looks at the data you have selected and chooses the row or column with the most data points for the data series in the chart. If row and column titles are selected, they also affect the way the data is plotted in the chart. The following activity will illustrate how selection can affect the chart.

ACTIVITY 10.4

Selecting Data for a Chart

1. Close any open spreadsheets.

2. Open CHARTS.WKS from the student diskette.

3. Select the data for the first chart.

    select the range C3:E7

    click the Chart icon

    click OK to create a chart

4. The data for the second chart is identical but arranged with the rows and columns reversed. Select the data for the second chart.

    choose Window, CHARTS.WKS to return to the spreadsheet

    select the range C9:G11

    click the Chart icon and click OK

    choose Window, Tile

    The charts are identical. Works has chosen the row or column with the greater number of data points, so in both cases you have two series, each with four data points (categories), rather than four series and two categories.

5. Close the second chart.

    double-click the Control-menu box in the second chart (Chart2 from CHARTS.WKS) to close it

6. Select data for the second chart again.

    select the range C9:G11

click the Chart icon

click the Down option button in the How is your spreadsheet organized? *area*

click OK

The data is now shown with two categories (West and East) and four data series (1st, 2nd, 3rd, and 4th).

7. Close both charts but leave the spreadsheet open for the next activity.

ACTIVITY 10.5

Selecting Labels

1. Create the first sine wave chart.

   select the range I3:J28

   click the Chart icon

   choose the Line chart in the What type of chart do you want? *list box*

   view the sample chart in the dialog box

   click OK

   The chart shows two data series, Phase and Amplitude, plotted on the same chart. However, the intent was a single data series with the Phase providing the intervals for the X-axis. If the column has a heading, Works assumes the column is a data series.

2. Create the second sine wave chart.

   select the range I3:J28

   click the Chart icon

   choose the Line chart in the What type of chart do you want? *list box*

   in the 3) First column contains: *option area click Category labels*

   Now the chart shows a single data series.

   click OK

   The chart now has a single data series. Amplitude is plotted as a function of phase.

3. Delete each of the charts (Works permits a maximum of eight charts to be attached to a spreadsheet). Leave CHARTS.WKS open for the next activity.

Adding Titles, Data Labels, and a Legend to a Chart

You can add a primary and secondary title to your chart as well as titles for each axis. The data in your chart can be labeled so individual members of a series are easy to pick out. A legend shows the names of the data series. Titles, labels, and a legend will enhance the information the chart is to convey. Although you can include a title when you create the chart, you can also change it or add a title later.

ACTIVITY 10.6
Adding Titles and a Legend

1. Make CHARTS.WKS the active spreadsheet.

2. Create a chart.

   select the range C3:E7

   click the Chart icon

   click OK

3. Add titles.

   choose Edit, Titles

   *type **Quarterly Sales** in the Chart Title box*

   *type **East and West Divisions** in the Subtitle box*

   *type **Quarter** in the Horizontal (X) Axis box*

   *type **Sales** in the Vertical (Y) Axis box*

   click OK

4. Format the Title font.

   click the chart title to select it

   choose Format, Font and Style

   make the Title font Arial, bold, 14 point

(elf

click OK, then click somewhere in the chart to deselect the title

choose Format, Font and Style

make the Subtitle and Labels font Arial, normal, 12 point

5. Add a legend.

   choose Format, Add Legend

   A check mark shows whether the Show Legend command is active.

6. Add a border if you like.

   choose Format, Add Border

   A check mark shows whether the Show Border command is active.

7. Delete all charts.

   choose Tools, Delete Charts

   click each chart in turn and then click Delete to delete each one

   when all charts have been deleted click OK

8. Leave the spreadsheet open for the next activity.

ACTIVITY 10.7
Data Labels

1. Create a chart.

   choose Window, CHARTS.WKS

   select the range E3:E7

   click the Chart icon

   select the 3-D Pie Chart and click OK

2. Add data labels.

   choose Window, Tile

   choose Edit, Data Labels

   click the Cell Contents option button in the 1st Label area

Spreadsheet

type **C4:C7** *in the* Cell Range *text box*

The range C4:C7 is the range in the spreadsheet containing the labels.

click the Percentages option button in the 2nd Label area

type **C4:C7** *in the* Cell Range *text box and click OK*

3. Delete all the charts attached to CHARTS.WKS and close the spreadsheet without saving the changes.

On Your Own

In this exercise you will create a line chart and experiment with the formatting options.

1. Open CHARTS.WKS from the student diskette.

2. Create a chart from the range I3:J28. In the *New Chart* dialog box:

    Choose Line chart.

    Type **Line Chart** as a title. In the *How is your spreadsheet data organized?* area mark the options buttons as follows:

    Which way do your series go? Down
    First row contains: Legend texts
    First column contains: Category labels

3. Reduce the frequency of the X-axis titles. Choose Format, Horizontal Axis. Type a label frequency of **3**.

4. Add X- and Y-axis titles. Choose Edit, Titles. Type **Phase** in the *Horizontal axis* text box and **Amplitude** in the *Vertical axis* text box.

5. Close the spreadsheet without saving changes.

Changing Scale and Adding Gridlines

By default, the vertical scale of a chart starts at zero and proceeds upward along the Y-axis to a value determined by the maximum value in the data series. With large values it is difficult to notice small differences in the members of a data series. You can change the scale to accentuate the differences. You can also add gridlines to help make comparisons about the relative magnitudes of the members.

ACTIVITY 10.8

Setting the Y-axis Scale and Adding Gridlines

1. Open or make CHARTS.WKS the active spreadsheet. Create a new chart and format the Y-axis titles.

   select the range C3:E7

   choose Format, Number and click the Currency option

   set the Number of Decimals to 0, then click OK

   click the Charts icon and click OK to create a bar chart

   The currency format is added to the Y-axis titles.

2. Change the scale.

   choose Format, Vertical Y-axis

   type **200000** *in the* Minimum *box and* **25000** *in the* Interval *box*

   mark the Show Gridlines check box and click OK

   The differences in the height of the bars is accentuated by the change in scale.

3. Add vertical gridlines.

   choose Format, Horizontal X-axis

   mark the Show Gridlines check box

4. Leave the chart active for the next activity.

Changing Colors and Patterns

By default Works selects a group of colors for your data markers, one color for each series. You can choose other colors and add patterns to the data markers if you wish. You may find later that other patterns will improve the quality of your printed charts. To see how the chart will look when printed choose View, Display as Printed.

Patterns and Colors dialog box

ACTIVITY 10.9

Colors and Patterns

1. Be sure the last chart you created is active or create a bar chart using the range C3:E7 in the CHARTS.WKS spreadsheet.

2. Add colors and patterns to the first series.

   choose Format, Patterns & Colors

   click the 1st option in the Series area

   select Blue in the Color area and Dense in the Patterns area

   click Format button to add the formats to the 1st series

   *do **not** click Close*

3. Add colors and patterns to the second series

   click the 2nd option in the Series area

   select Light Red in the Color area and scroll through the Patterns box to select // in the Patterns area

   click Format to add the formats to the 2nd series

   click Close to apply the formats to the chart

   The *Markers* list box is not available with bar or pie charts. With line charts you may select the markers for data points.

   choose View, Display as Printed to see how the printed chart will look

4. Delete all the charts and close the spreadsheet without saving the changes.

Printing

The data has been recorded, the formulas and functions have been entered, and the spreadsheet formatted. The charts have been created and their titles and legends and gridlines added. Now comes printing. When you print a spreadsheet Works will, by default, divide it into page-sized pieces and print them first from left to right, then down a page and left to right again, and continue until the entire spreadsheet is printed. You can define a range for Works to print, or you may choose where pages

are to break if you print more than one page. In addition, as you did in
the word processor, you can add headers and footers. If you print a chart,
you can decide how you want it to look as well.

To enter a page break, click the column label to the right, or the row label
below where you want the page break to occur. Choose Insert, Page
Break. To delete a page break, click as in the step above and choose
Insert, Delete Page Break.

ACTIVITY 10.10
Printing Part of a Spreadsheet

1. Open the spreadsheet INVEST.WKS from the student diskette.

2. Choose a range to print.

    select the range A3:D54

    choose Format, Set Print Area

    click OK to agree to set the print area to the current selection

3. Preview the printed output.

    click the Preview icon (looks like a page and magnifying glass)

    or

    choose File, Print Preview

    The last line of the print area has not been included.

    click Cancel

    choose File, Page Setup

    change the top and bottom margins to .5" and click OK

    review the page with Print Preview again and choose Cancel

4. Center the range on the page.

    choose File, Page Setup & Margins

    make the left margin 2" and click OK

    use Print Preview to view the page

5. Print the range.

    click the Print button in Print Preview

    or

    click Cancel and choose File, Print

    click OK to print the spreadsheet

6. Leave INVEST.WKS open for the next activity.

ACTIVITY 10.11

Printing an Entire Spreadsheet

1. Select the entire spreadsheet to print.

    click the rectangular box at the intersection of the row and column labels

    choose Format, Set Print Area

2. Change the font to a smaller size.

    *type **9** in the font size box*

    This is also a good way to zoom the spreadsheet if you would like to see a little more on each screen.

3. Reset the margins.

    choose File, Page Setup

    set the top, bottom, right, and left margins to 1"

4. Use Print, Preview to review how the spreadsheet will be printed.

    click the Print Preview icon

    use the Next and Previous page buttons to see how the pages will look when printed

5. Close the spreadsheet and do not save the changes.

Printing a Chart

Printing a chart is much like printing a spreadsheet except you print the entire chart without page breaks. You can also print both charts and spreadsheets in either portrait or landscape orientation. Because the computer screen is wider than it is long, your chart will look more like the screen if you print it in landscape orientation. Of course, you can use Print Preview to see how your chart will look.

- To print in landscape orientation you must change both Page Setup & Margins, and Printer Setup as you did when you printed a landscape page with the word processor.

- Some printers aren't capable of showing the various densities in the Patterns & Colors, Patterns box.

ACTIVITY 10.12
Printing Your Chart

1. Open the CHARTS.WKS spreadsheet from the student diskette.

2. Create a chart.

   select the range C3:E7 and click the Chart icon

   click OK to create the bar chart

3. Format the chart.

   choose View, Display as Printed

   choose Format and check Add Legend

   choose Edit, Titles

   *type **Quarterly Sales** in the* Chart Title *box*

   choose and check Format, Add Border

   choose Format, Patterns and Colors and choose ++ for the first series and xx *for the second series in the* Patterns *list box*

   click Close

   click the Print, Preview icon to view the chart

   Note that the chart is presented in portrait orientation.

   click Cancel

4. Print the chart in landscape orientation.

   choose File, Printer Setup

click the Setup button in the Printer Setup *dialog box*

click the Landscape orientation option

click the two OK buttons in the dialog boxes to return to your chart

choose File, Page Setup and click the Source, Size and Orientation tab

click the Landscape option to reverse the length and width of the paper

click OK

click the Print Preview button to review before printing

click the Print button in the Print Preview window

5. Reset the Printer Setup and Page Setup & Margins.

6. Close the spreadsheet without saving the changes.

Case Study

In this case study you will create a chart of the relationship between the term of a $10,000, 8 percent loan and the monthly payment over a range of 6 to 60 months at 6-month intervals.

1. Open the spreadsheet PMTSTUDY.WKS from the student diskette.

2. In cell C6 type **Payment** and in cell B7 type **6**.

3. In cell C7 enter the PMT() function using the input cells B3 and C3 and B7 as arguments. Don't forget to use the proper absolute and relative cell addresses, so that the function can be copied into a range.

4. Using cell B7, fill a series into the range B7:B16 with a step of 6.

5. Using cell C7, fill down into the range C7:C16. Format the range as currency with 0 decimal points.

6. Create a chart from the table using the range B6:C16. Set the chart type to line with Filled Box markers.

7. Add *Monthly Payments* as a title to the chart. Title the horizontal axis *Months* and the vertical axis *Payment*. As a Subtitle use *$10,000 at 8% for Various Terms*. Remove the legend from the bottom of the chart if one appears there.

8. Save the spreadsheet and chart with the name MYSTUDY.WKS. Print the chart with a landscape orientation.

    Optional: On the same spreadsheet, create a table and chart relating the values of the radius, area, and volume of a sphere.

Area = $4*PI*R^2$

Volume = $4/3*PI*R^3$, where R is the radius of the sphere and PI is the ratio of the circumference to the radius of a circle, 3.14159. The range B25:D37 will give you a start.

Hint: You can use the value of the PI() function to return the value of PI. See cell C25. Plot your graph both linearly and logarithmically.

Quick Check

. Name as many chart parts as you can remember.

. Which charting commands do you use to:

add titles?

change the scale of the vertical axis?

change the color of a data series?

change the type and format of a chart?

add gridlines?

add a border? a legend?

preview a chart?

Spreadsheet

3. How do you print a chart with a landscape orientation? What should you remember after you have printed such a chart?

4. How does Works choose which rows or columns will compose the data series in a chart and which will provide the number of data points in a series?

Part III
The Database Program

In This Section

❏ *Start the Database program*

❏ *Understand how to organize data for a database*

❏ *Create and edit a database form*

❏ *Add, edit, format, and delete data in a database*

❏ *Use mathematical formulas and functions*

❏ *Search a database for data meeting your criteria*

❏ *Sort a database alphabetically or numerically*

❏ *Use a database to create a report*

Database

Building a Database

11

Overview

With the Works 3.0 for Windows database program you can create a form and then enter data for a mailing list, a stamp collection, an inventory, or any kind of information you want to organize. Once the data has been added to the database you can sort it alphabetically or numerically. You can also retrieve data that you need very quickly. If you like, you can create reports, printing the database data as shown in the database or grouped by categories.

The database can also be used with the word processor to create form letters (mail merge). When the form letters are printed, information from the database is substituted in appropriate places to create individualized letters.

Objectives

- Learn what a database is
- Understand the structure of a database
- Create a database form
- Add data to a database
- Edit the data
- Modify the database form
- Use formulas to calculate values in the database

What Is a Database?

A **database** is a collection of organized information or data. A telephone book is a good example. There, the data consists of the names, addresses, and telephone numbers of everyone having a listed telephone. The data is arranged by individuals with all the information pertaining to a single individual collected in one place.

Record—In a telephone book, the information regarding each individual is placed on a separate line. In a database, the data for an individual (or account receivable, or inventory item, or stamp, or coin, etc.) is called a record. Each record is automatically assigned a number.

Field—Each record is divided into fields. In the telephone book the fields might be the name, the address, and the telephone number of individuals in the book. Each field receives a name.

How to Divide a Record into Fields

The manner in which you divide a record into fields is determined by how you plan to use the data. For example, the database below has two records. The information in each record is similar in arrangement but different in content. Each record must have the information entered in the same order. For the two records, the order is name, address, and telephone number.

Each record has been divided into fields: a NAME field, then an ADDRESS field, and finally a TELEPHONE field. The number of fields and the order in which they appear is chosen by the creator of the database. A single piece of information can be found within the database by referring to the field name and the record number. Anne Robinson's address is found in the ADDRESS field of record 2.

Name	Address	Telephone
Albert Williams	234 Front St., Frontier, OR 23456	(812) 341-2234
Anne Robinson	169 Ferndale Dr., Apt 4, Westview, IN 41322	(815) 664-9071

The structure of the records shown above is too rigid to allow much flexibility when you get ready to use the database. You could not sort alphabetically by the last name because the sorting process uses the order of text as it appears in a field and the name field begins with the first name. Thus you can only sort on the first name. A better arrangement for the fields in the two records would be like this:

Last Name	First Name	Address	City	St	Zip	Telephone
Williams	Albert	234 Front St.	Frontier	OR	23456	(812) 341-2234
Robinson	Anne	169 Ferndale Dr., Apt 4	Westview	IN	41322	(815) 664-9071

Each item in a record that might serve as a key for sorting or searching is assigned to a different field. In addition, unique field names are used to designate each field.

Even the arrangement of fields shown above has limitations. For example, perhaps you would later like to use the database for a merge mailing. The heads of the letters might look like the ones below:

Ms. Anne Robinson   Mr. Albert Williams
169 Ferndale Dr., Apt 4   234 Front St.
Westview, IN 41322   Frontier, OR 23456

Dear Ms. Robinson,   Dear Al,

Unless you add a field containing the individual's title (such as Ms., Mr., or Dr.) you won't be able to include it in the address. Likewise, if you don't add a field containing a salutation, you will not be able to address Mr. Williams as Al. Fields can be added to a database later, but the best idea is to first thoroughly think through how the information in your database will be used. Choose the fields based on the broadest use you can think of. It is generally better to divide the record into too many fields than too few. For example, you might include a birthday field so you can mail birthday cards to Al and Ms. Robinson the week before their birthdays.

In addition to a name, each field is given a length. The length is equal to the maximum number of characters you expect to use if it is a text field or the greatest number of significant figures if it is a number field.

Some facts about database fields and records:

- You may have as many as 32,000 records.

- A field name can consist of up to 15 characters, including spaces, but cannot include the single quote ('). You can have up to 256 fields, and each can hold 256 characters.

Creating a Database

The first step in creating a database is to tell the Works 3.0 for Windows database program the name and size of each field that is to be included in a record. When you start the database program, Works displays a blank form for you to define and add fields and field names to. The database is shown in Form view. After the form has been filled out it might look like the one on the next page.

Database

```
┌─────────────────────────────────────────────────────────────────────┐
│ ─              Microsoft Works - [Data1]                      ▼  ▲   │
│ ─  File  Edit  View  Insert  Format  Tools  Window  Help            ♦ │
│ Times New Roman  ±  12  ±  [icons]                                    │
│ X4.50" Y2.00"                                                         │
│                                                                    ▲  │
│                    DSR Customer Database                              │
│                                                                       │
│     Last Name: ..............................                         │
│                                                                       │
│     First Name: ............................                          │
│                                                                       │
│     Address: ..............................                           │
│                                                                       │
│     City: ................   State: ......   ZIP: ...............     │
│                                                                       │
│                                                                       │
│           Title: ..............   Salutation: ................        │
│                                                                       │
│                                                                       │
│                      Birthday: ............   (if known)             │
│                                                                    ▼  │
│ |◄ ◄ Record 1 ► ►| ◄                                              ►   │
│ ALT for commands; F2 to edit; CTRL+PGDN/UP for next record. │Pg1│NUM│1│0/0│
└─────────────────────────────────────────────────────────────────────┘
```

The database form screen has two purposes. First, you can use it to create your database by adding fields and telling Works the length of each field. Second, you can use it to view the information in the database as each record is shown on a copy of the form. When your information is displayed in this way you are viewing it in Form view.

After you have decided what information you want to include in each record, how you want the records divided into fields, and how large each field should be, it is time to begin.

• In Works, choose File, Create New File and choose the database icon.

• Click in the blank form where you want the first field name to appear.

• Type the field name followed by a colon (:).

• In the *Field Size* dialog box type the length of the field in the *Width* text box. If you want more than one line of that width, type the number of lines in the *Height* box. Press [Enter] to add the field to the form (record). The name of the field appears dimmed in the dialog box.

```
┌───────────────────────────────────────┐
│ ─              Field Size              │
│                                        │
│  Type a width that will best fit your  │
│  entries. Type a new height if you     │  ┌──────┐
│  want a multi-line field.              │  │  OK  │
│                                        │  └──────┘
│                                        │  ┌────────┐
│   Name:  [Name        ]                │  │ Cancel │
│                                        │  └────────┘
│   Width: [20]                          │  ┌──────┐
│                                        │  │ Help │
│   Height: [1]                          │  └──────┘
└───────────────────────────────────────┘
```

In the next activity you will build a database for a coin collection. Don't worry about the exact placement of fields; you can move them later if you wish. The field names and lengths are:

Coin Type:	8
Year:	6
Mint:	2
Condition:	12
Cost:	6
Date Acquired:	10
Comments:	15 on each of two lines (type 2 in the *Height* box)

ACTIVITY 11.1
Creating a Database Form

1. Start Works 3.0 for Windows.

2. Open the database program and create a database.

    if you see the Startup *box on screen, click the Database button*

    or

    choose File, Create New File and click Database

    The database program opens, displaying a blank form . The insertion point is positioned in the upper left corner of the screen.

3. Add a field.

    type **Coin Type:** *(don't forget the colon)*

    press ENTER

    type **8** *in the* Width *box*

    click OK or press ENTER

    The field is entered with a dotted line, which indicates the width of the field. The insertion point moves to the next line.

Database

4. Add the second field.

    type **Year:**

    press

    type **6** *as the width*

    press

5. Add the rest of the fields to the database in a similar fashion.

    Mint: 2

    Condition: 12

    Cost: 6

    Date Acquired: 10

    Comments: 15 on each of two lines (type 2 in the *Height* box)

6. Save the database.

    choose File, Save As

    type **MYCOINS** *in the* File Name *text box*

    select the A: drive (or the drive where you are saving your files)

    press *to save the file*

    Works add the extension .WDB to the file name. Leave the database open for the next activity.

Adding Data to the Database

To add information to a database, select (highlight) the field and type the data.

-   To select a field with the mouse, click the mouse pointer on the dotted line following the field name where you want to enter data.

-   To select a field with the keyboard, press [Tab] to go to the next field or [Shift] [Tab] to go to the previous field.

- If your form is larger than one screen use the scroll bars or press [Page Down] and [Page Up] to move to the other part of the form.

- When you finish with a record, press [Tab] while in the last field or [Ctrl] [Page Down] while in any field to move to the next record. Press [Ctrl] [Page Up] to go to the previous record.

- If you are using the mouse you can click the Next Record or Previous Record arrows at the left end of the scroll bar. Be careful to differentiate between Next Record and Go to the End of the database and Previous Record and Go to the Beginning of the database.

ACTIVITY 11.2
Entering Data in a Database

1. Enter the first coin type.

    click just above the dotted line following the field name Coin Type

    The data entry area is selected (highlighted).

    type **Penny** *in the Coin Type field*

    press TAB

    type **1924** *in the Year field*

    press TAB

    type **D** *in the Mint field*

    press TAB

    type **Xtra Fine** *in the Condition field*

    press TAB

    type **40.00** *in the Cost field*

    press TAB

    type **3/16/93** *in the Date Acquired field*

    press TAB

Database

type **Good buy**

press TAB *to move on to the next record*

2. Enter the data for the second record.

    repeat the steps for the second record, the nickel coin

3. Complete the data entry with the third and fourth records.

    press TAB *to skip a blank field*

4. Save and close the database.

    press CTRL S

    choose File, Close

Coin Type:	Penny	Nickel	Dime	Penny
Year:	1924	1935	1928	1943
Mint:	D	P	S	P
Condition:	Xtra Fine	Unc	Very Fine	Unc
Cost:	40.00	8.00	5.00	1.20
Date Acquired:	3/16/93	3/16/93	4/21/93	3/11/91
Comments:	Good buy	Found in change		Zinc-coated steel

Form View

You can easily edit your database in Form view using methods similar to those in the word processor and spreadsheet programs.

• To move around within a form, press [Tab] to go to the next field or [Shift] [Tab] to go to the previous field. The active field is highlighted (selected). You can also click the field.

• To move within the database, use the mouse to click the Next Record or Previous Record arrows at the left end of the scroll bar. Be careful to differentiate between Next Record and Go to the End of the database and Previous Record and Go to the Beginning of the database. In Form view, the vertical scroll bar is used to scroll through a single record rather than moving through the database.

(elf)

- With the keyboard press [Ctrl] [Page Down] to go to the next record or [Ctrl] [Page Up] to go to the previous record. [Ctrl] [Home] goes to the first record, and [Ctrl] [End] goes to the next record beyond the end of the database. Use [Ctrl] [End] to add a record to the database.

- Choose Edit, Go To or press [F5], then type a record number in the *Go To* box to go to a specific record number.

- You can tell which record is active by looking at the left end of the Status bar. The record number is shown between the Previous Record and Next Record arrows (the word NUM means that you have your [Num Lock] key activated).

ACTIVITY 11.3
Moving Around in Form View

1. Open the database ATLAS.WDB from the student diskette.

2. Use Form view.

   choose View, Form and make sure Form is checked

3. Use the keyboard to browse the database.

   press [CTRL] [PG↓] *twice to go to record 3*

   note the number in the Status bar

   press [CTRL] [PG↓] *until you arrive at record 11*

   press [CTRL] [PG↑] *to go to the previous record*

   press [CTRL] [HOME] *to go to the beginning of the database*

4. Go to the Area field of record 14.

   choose Edit, Go To

   type **14** *in the* Go To *box*

   click OK

   choose Edit, Go To and click Area in the Names *box*

   click OK

5.   Move within the form.

press **[SHIFT]** **[TAB]** *until you get to the State field*

6.   Leave the database open for the next activity.

Editing in Form View

As you might expect, simple editing is done in much the same way as with word processing and the spreadsheet program.

•   To edit a field, click on it and then either type over the present data or press [F2] to edit the field in the Formula bar.

CAUTION: Always save your work before you delete a field or record so you can restore the data if you need to. Be sure that you really want to delete a field or record before you do so.

•   To delete a record, choose Edit, Cut Record. Be careful. Although the record is in the clipboard, once you have used Cut or Copy again, the record is unrecoverable.

•   To delete a field entry, select the data and choose Edit, Clear Field Entry or press [Delete]. You cannot paste back a field entry that has been cleared.

CAUTION: There is a vast difference between deleting a field entry and deleting a field. Deleting an entry erases only the data for that field in a single record. Deleting a field removes the field and all the corresponding data from the entire database.

•   To insert a new field, click on an empty part of the database form. Type a field name followed by a colon and choose a width and height.

•   To insert a new record, move through the database to the location where you want to add a record. Choose Insert, Record. The remaining records will follow the record you inserted. If you want to append a record to the end of the database, press [Ctrl] [End] and enter the data for the new record.

ACTIVITY 11.4
Editing in Form View

1.   Make ATLAS.WDB the active database.

2.   Delete a field entry.

move to record 27

click in the entry for the Population field (NOT the field name)

choose Edit, Clear Field Entry

3. Delete a record.

    move to record 14 (Texas) and note in the Status bar that there are 50 records

    choose Edit, Cut Record

    Look at the right end of the Status bar and note that there are now 49 records in the database.

4. Copy the record back in a new location.

    move to record 19

    choose Edit, Paste Record

    confirm that the record is now between original records 18 and 19 as shown by the No. field at the top of each record.

5. Insert a blank record.

    move to record 5

    choose Insert, Record

    type the data below into the new record

No.: **51**	*State:* **District of Columbia**
Abv.: **DC**	
Capital: **Washington**	*E/W:* **E**
Area: **69**	
Population: **615,000**	*Highest El:* **410**

6. Save the database with the name MYATLAS.WDB and leave it open for the next activity.

Modifying the Appearance of Form View

You can improve the appearance of your form by arranging the fields and adding titles and comments.

*   You can change the location of the fields in Form view by dragging them to a new location. If you click on a field or field entry, the pointer changes to a drag arrow, which you can use to drag the field.

The X and Y positions of a selected field are shown at the left end of the Formula bar. The positions are measured from the edge of the paper they would be printed on.

- If the entry field is too short you will see a series of pound signs (####). You can change the field length by choosing Format, Field Size. You can use the mouse to do the same job by clicking in the field entry area. Three lighter squares appear on the bottom and right sides of the selection and at the lower right corner. When the pointer is over the square, the word Drag appears. Drag a square to change the length of the field or to change it to multiple lines. These changes will affect every record.

- If you want to add a title or a comment to the form, click where the comment is to appear, type the comment (or title), and press [Enter]. Do *not* follow a comment with a colon.

- To help you align fields, Works provides a Snap to Grid command in the Format menu. This will cause fields to jump into position as you move them. This feature can be turned off if you wish.

ACTIVITY 11.5

Improving the Appearance of the Form

1. Make MYATLAS.WDB the active database.

2. Drag the fields into the approximate locations shown above.

   Hint: Drag the bottom fields down first, to make room for the title.

3. Add a title and comment as shown.

   click at the top of the screen and type **DSR Atlas of the USA**

   with the title selected choose Format, Font and Style

   make the title Arial, bold, 18 point

   click at the right of the Population field and type the comment **(1989)** *(include the parentheses)*

   with the comment selected, click the Italic icon

4. Save and close the MYATLAS database.

On Your Own

Create a database form like the one shown below.

```
EMPLOYEE.WDB
┌──────────────────────────────────────────────┐
│           DSR Employee Database                │
│                                                │
│   Last Name: _____        First Name: _____ │
│                                                │
│   Home Address: _____                   │
│                                                │
│   City: _____      State: ___    Zip: _____   │
│                                                │
│               Employee No.: ____               │
│               Date Started: ____               │
│               Department: _____                │
│                                                │
│ │◄ ◄ Record 1 ► ►│ ◄                           │
└──────────────────────────────────────────────┘
```

1. Open a database form.

2. Add the fields. Use the field names and widths (in parentheses) as shown below.

3. Move the fields to the approximate locations shown.

4. Add the title. Format it bold.

5. Add two employees to the database.

Last Name: (20)	Fletcher	Thompson
First Name: (15)	Andrea	William
Home Address: (25)	234 First St., Apt. 4A	303 South Cornell Circle
City: (20)	Bethesda	Chevy Chase
State: (3)	MD	MD
Zip: (8)	31426	31428
Employee No.: (5)	37	83
Date Started: (8)	11/14/72	3/6/87
Department: (12)	Legal	Contracts

6. Save the database with the name EMPLOYEE.WDB. Close the database.

Database

List View

So far you have been working with Form view where each record is displayed on a single screen. To view a list of the records, switch to List view. List view displays the records in a form similar to a spreadsheet. Each row represents a record and each column a field, headed by a field name.

To switch to List view, click the List icon or choose View, List from the menu. The List icon is the second from the right in the group of four to the right of the **U** underline icon. While in List view you will find that many editing and formatting tasks you did with a spreadsheet are similar. For example:

- To widen or narrow a field, drag the right edge of the field name in the label row to the right or left. For a best fit choose Format, Field Width and mark the Best Fit check box.

- To delete the contents of a field, click the field and press [Delete], or choose Edit, Clear Field Entry.

- To delete a field (column), click the field label. The entire column is selected. Choose Edit, Delete Record/Field.

CAUTION: The cautions regarding the deletion of records and fields in Form view apply here as well.

To delete a record (row), click the record number. The entire row is selected. Choose Edit, Delete Record/Field.

To add a field (column), click the field label where you want the column to appear. Choose Edit, Insert Record/Field. The new column will appear at the selected position and will push the present columns to the right as necessary. Then choose Edit, Field Name and give the field a name **without** a trailing colon. Choose Format, Field Width to change the width of the column.

To add a record (row), click the row label where you want the row to appear. Choose Edit, Insert Record/Field. The new row will push the present rows down as necessary.

ACTIVITY 11.6

Editing a Database in List View

1.   Open the database COINS.WDB from the student diskette.

2. Change to List view.

    click the List icon or choose View, List

3. Scroll through the list of coins.

    click the down arrow in the vertical scroll bar to scroll through the database

    press PG↑ *to move up in the database*

    press CTRL END *and* CTRL HOME *to move to the end and beginning of the database*

4. Delete the empty record.

    click on record label number 7 at the left edge of the database

    The entire record is selected.

    choose Insert, Delete Record/Field

5. Rename a field.

    click the column label named Date Acquired

    choose Edit, Field Name

    shorten the field name by typing **Date Acqd.** *in the* Name *text box and click OK*

6. Add a field.

    click the column label named Comments

    choose Insert, Record/Field

    choose Edit, Field Name and type **Value Now** *in the* Name *text box*

    click OK to add the field and push the remaining field to the right

7. Widen the field.

    drag the right border of the field label to the right until the field name shows

    narrow or widen the rest of the fields to match their values or field labels

Database

8. Add data to the new Value Now field.

   type **43.5** *in record 1*

   type **10** *in record 2*

   type **6.25** *in record 3*

9. Change the value in a field.

   type **13.5** *in the Cost field of record 6*

10. Return to Form view.

    choose View, Form or click the Form icon

11. Drag the new field.

    click on the Value Now field at the top of the form

    drag it to a location beside the Cost field

12. Leave the database open for the next activity.

Moving Fields and Records

You may want to move fields or records to bring data closer together for comparison.

- To move a field in List view, click the field label to select the field throughout the database. Choose Edit, Cut to move the column of data to the Clipboard. Click the field label where you want the column to appear and choose Edit, Paste.

- In Form view you can move the field by dragging.

- To move a record in List view, click the record label (number) and choose Edit, Cut. Click the record label where you want the record to appear and choose Edit, Paste.

- In Form view you can move a record by going to it and choosing Edit, Cut Record. Next, go to where you want the record to appear and choose Edit, Paste Record.

- You can move more than one field or record at a time in List view by selecting adjacent fields or records first and then cutting and pasting.

ACTIVITY 11.7

Moving a Field in List View

1. Make COINS.WDB the active database.

2. Change your view to List view.

   click the List icon

3. Select the field to move.

   click on the Value Now label to select the entire column

4. Move the field to a new location.

   choose Edit, Cut

   click on the Date Acqd. label

   choose Edit, Paste

5. Leave the database open for the next activity.

ACTIVITY 11.8

Moving a Record in Form View

1. Change to Form view.

   click the Form icon

2. Select a record to move.

   press *and type* **5**

   press ENTER

   choose Edit, Cut Record

3. Move the record.

   press *and type* **19**

   press ENTER

   choose Edit, Paste Record

The record is pasted from the Clipboard as record 19 in the database. Following records are moved down.

4.   Leave the database open for the next activity.

Formatting a Database

You've already learned to change the width of a field or column and to change the font of a title. In fact, formatting in your database is much like formatting in a spreadsheet. There are significant differences, however.

*   If you change the format of a single field entry, all the entries for that field throughout the database are changed as well. This applies to style (bold, italic, underline), alignment (left, center, right), and to date and numeric formats.

*   In a manner similar to the spreadsheet program, if you enter a date in a form that Works recognizes as a date, it will be given a short date format. The same reasoning applies to times.

*   Numeric values are initially entered with a general format. If a value is too large for a field it shows as #####. Widen the field to view the number.

*   You may format a field by choosing a style or alignment icon, or by choosing a numeric format from the Format menu. You may also choose a font and point size, but these will apply to the entire database (choose a smaller size to see more of the database at one time).

ACTIVITY 11.9

Formatting a Database

1.   Make sure COINS.WDB is still the active database.

2.   Center a field.

   change to List view

   press CTRL HOME *to go to the top of the database*

   click a field in the Mint column (or the Mint field label)

   choose Format, Alignment

   click the Center option button

   click OK

3. Format currency.

click a field in the Cost column

choose Format, Number

click the Currency option button

*type **2** in the* Number of decimals *box*

click OK

4. Format the dates.

click a field in the Date Acqd. column

choose Format, Numbers

click the Date option button

choose the long format (for example, May 24, 1994) in the Date *list box*

click OK

choose Format, Field Width and click the Best Fit check box

5. Save and close the database.

Adding a Picture to Form View

You can add clipart in the Form view of your database in much the same way you placed a picture of a blue sedan in the DSR newsletter.

- Choose Form view and click where you want the picture.

- Choose Insert, ClipArt and select a picture from the ClipArt Gallery.

- Size and shape the picture with the eight drag handles.

Coin Collection

Coin Type: **Dime**

Year: 1928   Mint: S

Condition: Very Fine   Cost: $5.00

Date Acquired: April 21, 1993

Comments: Found in
change

ACTIVITY 11.10

Adding ClipArt

1. Open the database COINSFO.WDB.

2. Select a place for the clipart.

    click in the open area in the upper right portion of the form

3. Add the picture.

    choose Insert, ClipArt

    in the Gallery double-click one of the pictures

    The picture appears in the database form.

4. Size, shape, and move the clipart.

    select the picture

    choose Format, Picture/Object

    in the Scaling area of the dialog box type **80** *in both the* Width *and* Height *boxes*

    The Size area values change accordingly.

5. Add a border.

    choose Format, Border

    click the double-line border

    click OK

6. Close the database and do not save the changes.

On Your Own

1. Open the ATLAS.WDB database from the student diskette.

2. In Form view arrange the fields in an attractive manner. Group similar information.

3. In List view, widen the fields so you can see the field names.

4. Center align the No., Abv., and E/W fields.

5. Apply a Comma format with 0 decimal places to the numeric fields.

6. Make the State field bold.

7. Move the record for Oregon from row (record) 4 to record 11.

8. Move the Area field after the Population field.

9. Close the database without saving the changes.

Quick Check

1. In your own words, define the nature of a database. What is a record? What is a field?

2. What is the difference between Form view and List view?

3. List three ways to change the width of a field. Can you change the width of the field name in List view without using the menu?

4. Name the steps in moving a field and a record.

5. How can you add a record in a database? a field?

6. What do the various icons on the Toolbar mean? Point to each to see its meaning.

Using a Database

12

Overview

The real purpose in building a database is so you can use it. You can add formulas and functions so that the Works for Windows 3.0 database program will make calculations for you. You can sort the data alphabetically, numerically, and by date, and you can find and compare data.

Objectives

- Have Works fill in parts of the database for you

- Use formulas and functions in database fields to make calculations

- Sort the database by fields, alphabetically, numerically, or by date

- Search the database for records containing information that meet criteria you specify

Entering the Same Data into a Field for Every Record

If you type an equal sign plus text enclosed in double quotes in any field, every record will be automatically filled with that text for that field. This is a simple way to save a lot of typing. For example, if you place =**"PA"** in a field where the postal abbreviation for Pennsylvania would be the most likely to be entered, you won't have to type it in the rest of the fields. You can type another value in the field if you have a few other states represented (without the "=). If you want to enter a number, leave out the double quote, for example, =**$5**.

ACTIVITY 12.1

Filling in a Field Automatically

1. Open the COINS.WDB database from the student diskette.

Database

2. Insert a field and give it a name.

   change to List view

   click on the field name Condition

   choose Insert, Record/Field

   or

   click the Insert Field icon (the second one to the left of the Help question mark)

   choose Edit, Field Name

   *type **Country** in the Name box and click OK*

3. Fill in each field in the Country column.

   type ="US" in the Country field of any record in the database that has other data present

   The field is filled throughout the database with the result of the formula.

4. Change a field.

   go to record 23

   *type **Can** in the Country field to override the default value of US*

5. Clear a formula.

   click the Country field label

   choose Edit, Clear Formula

   The fields are cleared, except for *Can*, but the label remains.

6. Add an entry to a selected number of records.

   *type **US** in the Country field for the first record in the database*

   in the Country field, drag from record 1 through record 10

   choose Edit, Fill Down

7. Close the database and do not save the changes.

elf

Using Formulas and Functions to Calculate Fields

You can use many of the same formulas and functions that you used in the spreadsheet program to calculate fields in a database.

- You can use a formula t calculate a value based on other fields. For example, if you have a field named Sum and two other fields named Cost and Tax, you can have the sum automatically calculated. In the Sum field type **=Cost+Tax**.

- You can even use functions. The sum function would look like this: =SUM(TEST 1, TEST 2, TEST 3) where TEST 1, TEST 2, and TEST 3 are the fields you want summed.

The DSR Atlas has been updated for the following activity.

ACTIVITY 12.2

Using a Formula in a Database

1. Open the ATLASPOP.WDB database from the student diskette.

2. Move the Max El field immediately to the right of the Area field.

   click on the field name at the top of the Max El column

   choose Edit, Cut

   click on the field name at the top of the Pop 1980 column

   choose Edit, Paste

3. Create a field.

   click the empty label to the right of the Pop Now label

   choose Edit, Field Name

   type **Change** *in the* Name *box and click OK*

4. Enter a formula in the field.

   in the Change field for one of the records type **=Pop Now-Pop 1980**

   A value for the change in population appears in each record.

5. Leave the database open for the next activity.

Summing the Fields in a Column

You can use a function to calculate a result based on the values of other fields in the same record, for example, =SUM(TEST 1, TEST 2, TEST 3) where TEST 1, TEST 2, and TEST 3 are the fields you want summed. You cannot, however, use the SUM() function at the bottom of a column to calculate the total of the fields in that column as you did with a spreadsheet. But you can calculate a running total in a field designed for that purpose. For example, using the DSR Atlas, you want to find the total population of the United States. In a new field that you might call Total, enter the formula **=Total+Pop Now**. In a spreadsheet, such an action would result in a circular error, using a cell address in a formula placed in that same cell. In the database program, the calculation uses the result from the field in the previous record.

ACTIVITY 12.3

Calculating a Running Total

1. Create a field.

    click the empty column label to the right of the Change label

    choose Edit, Field Name and type **Total** *in the* Name *box*

    click OK

2. Enter a formula to calculate a running total.

    type **=Total+Pop Now** *in the Total field of any record (except a blank record)*

    The Total field for each record is filled with the Total from the field in the record above plus the Pop Now field in the present record. In the Total field at the bottom of the database is the total population for the United States from the 1990 census, 249,024,940.

3. Close the database and do not save the changes.

ACTIVITY 12.4

Using a Function in a Database

1. Open the TESTAVG.WDB database from the student diskette.

2. Enter a function to find the average test score for each student.

    click the Average field in record 1

3. Use pointing to enter the function.

start typing the function **=AVG(**

click in the Test 1 column

type **,** *(a comma)*

click in the Test 2 column

type **,** *(a comma)*

click in the Test 3 column

type the closing **)**

Your formula should now read =AVG(Test 1, Test 2, Test 3).

press

Each record shows the average of the three tests for each student in the Average field. Note that the three arguments are field names separated by commas. You cannot use a similar technique to find the class average for each test using the AVG() function. You could find a running total for each test and then divide by 10.

4. Close the database and do not save the changes.

On Your Own

1. Open the ATLASPOP.WDB database.

2. Create a Density field by clicking an empty field label and giving it the name Density.

3. In the Density field enter a formula that will calculate the population density using the Pop Now and Area fields (density = population / area). Give the field a Comma format with 1 decimal place.

4. Create a Change field and enter a formula that will show the change in population between 1980 and now for each state.

5. Find the total change in population using a new field, Tot Change, that calculates a running total. Don't cheat by using a calculator or the spreadsheet program.

6. Close the database without saving the changes (or save the changes with a new name).

Database

Sorting a Database

One of the most important tasks appropriate for Works 3.0 is sorting the records of a database into alphabetical or numerical order. If you were working with an employee database, you might want to sort the records on:

- The last name, for an employee telephone directory.

- The zip code, for creating mailing labels. The Post Office requires a zip code sort for bulk mailings.

- The date the employees started to work so you could find the worker who had been with the company longest.

When you sort a database it will be on the basis of the contents of a particular field, called a key field. The sort may be made in either ascending order (A first, Z last or smaller numbers first, larger numbers last), or the opposite, descending order. If you have duplicate values in the key field of more than one record (two people with the last name Brown, for example), you can sort on a second key field (first name). The second sort will be carried out only within the duplicate records (same last name). Works lets you use as many as three keys.

- Using a secondary key field is the same as sorting twice. For example, in the case of names, you could first sort on the basis of the first name field. After the database was in order by first name, the database would be sorted by last name. Any duplicate last names would already have first names in order from the first sort.

- Sometimes you'll add key fields to a database solely to group records. Zip codes would be an example. In the ATLAS.WDB database, an E/W field was added so the database could be sorted into two groups, those east of the Mississippi River, and those to the west. This type of use is important to consider when designing the database.

To sort a database, choose Tools, Sort Records. Type the names of the key fields into the *1st Field*, *2nd Field*, and *3rd Field* text boxes (only the 1st Field is required). Finally, choose an Ascending or Descending option for each key field.

ACTIVITY 12.5

Sorting a Database

1. Open the ATLASPOP.WDB from the student diskette.

2. Sort the database alphabetically by state name.

choose Tools, Sort Records

type **State** *in the* 1st Field *text box (upper or lower case)*

choose the Ascend option and click OK

The database is sorted from Alabama to Wyoming.

3. Sort the database by population.

choose Tools, Sort Records

choose Pop Now in the 1st Field *list box*

choose the Ascend option and click OK

4. Group the states by east or west of the Mississippi River.

choose Tools, Sort Records

choose E/W in the 1st Field *list box*

choose the Descend option and click OK

5. Close the database and do not save the changes.

ACTIVITY 12.6
●Sorting with a Secondary Key

1. Open the REALTYDB.WDB database from the student diskette.

2. Sort the database by subdivision.

choose Tools, Sort Records

choose Subdivision for the 1st Field

choose the Ascend option and click OK

Note that the prices with each subdivision group are listed in random order.

3. Sort on price as the secondary key.

choose Tools, Sort Records

Subdivision should already show in the 1st Field *text box; if not, choose it*

choose Price for the 2nd Field

Database

choose the Ascending option

click OK

Note that the prices are now in ascending order within each subdivision group.

4. Sort the database on 1st Field—Subdivision, 2nd Field—Bedrooms, and 3rd Field—Baths.

5. Close the database and do not save the changes.

On Your Own

1. Open the ATLASPOP.WDB database from the student diskette.

2. Find the state with the highest mountain (Max El).

3. Find the state with the lowest populations density. Hint: You will have to create a density field first.

4. What is the state with the largest population west of the Mississippi? east of the Mississippi?

5. Which state has had the largest population gain since 1980? the largest loss?

6. Close the database and do not save the changes.

Searching a Database

There may be occasions when you want to find records that contain specific information such as a last name. This is what you do when you look up a name in a telephone directory. But what would you do if you wanted to find the name that belonged to a known telephone number? If you had to do it with a telephone book it would be a tedious process, but with a database you can easily search for information from any field. This is another important fact to keep in mind when you design your data form.

The easiest way to search is with the Find command:

*   Choose Edit, Find from the menu in either Form or List view. In the *Find What* text box type the text or value that you're looking for. If you choose the Next Record option, Works finds the next occurrence of the search text while all the records in the database are displayed. If you choose All Records, only the records containing the search text will be displayed.

- Searches are only conducted among records that are currently not hidden. If you chose All Records in a previous search, only the unhidden records found by the search will be shown. If you want to search all records, choose View, Show All Records first.

- The Find command searches for any text that matches what is typed in the _Find What_ box even if it's embedded within other text.

- You can use the * and ? wild cards with the Find command. A question mark stands for any character in the same position within the text. For example, _re?d_ stands for both _read_ and _reed_. The asterisk stands for any group of characters in that position. For example, _r*d_ stands for _read_ and _reed_ as before but also _rapid_, _Richard_, and _rancid_. In addition, because the search is not confined to whole words, you will find _tried_ and _treading_.

- To repeat a search, press [F7].

- To find the records that were not included, choose View, Switch Hidden Records, or, to show all records, choose View, Show All Records.

- The number of records that contain the search text or number is shown at the right end of the Status bar if you choose All Records in the _Find_ dialog box. A display of 8/50 means eight records were found in a 50-record database.

ACTIVITY 12.7
Searching for Specific Data in a Database

1. Open the ATLASPOP.WDB database from the student diskette.

2. Find Indiana.

   click the Form view icon

   choose View, Find

   type **Indiana** _in the_ Find What _text box and choose the Next Record option_

   The record for the state of Indiana appears on screen. The word _Indiana_ is highlighted in the State entry field.

   choose View, Find a second time and click OK

   The highlight jumps to the Capital field and the word _Indianapolis_ which contains the word _Indiana_.

Database

3.   Find Alabama.

choose Edit, Find

type **AL** *in the* Find What *text box and choose the All Records option*

Works finds Alaska instead.

click the List view icon

Eight records are shown. Each record has the letters *AL* somewhere within it, for example, *Salem*, the capital of Oregon.

choose Edit, Find

type **Alab** *in the* Find What *text box and choose the All Records option*

This time the search is unique—only Alabama is found.

4.   Leave the ATLASPOP.WDB database open for the next activity.

ACTIVITY 12.8

Using a Wild Card with a Search

1.   Find all the state names, capitals, and abbreviations that contain the letters *C* and *A* with a single letter between them.

choose Edit, Find with the All Records option

type **C?A** *in the* Find What *text box (finds 2 states)*

The first record is found because of **Cha**rleston, C?arleston; the second record because of Sa**cra**mento, Sac?amento.

2.   Find all the state names, capitals, and abbreviations that have a *C* and an *A* with any number of intervening letters.

choose View, Find with the All Records option

type **C*A** *in the* Find What *text box*

The search locates seven records.

The first record is found because of **Ca**rson City, **C*a**rson City. In this case the * stands for no character; the C and A together are enough. The second record is found because of **Cha**rleston, **C*a**rleston. In this case the * stands for the letter *h*. The third record is found because of **Colora**do, **C*a**do. Here the * stands for the letters *olor*.

3.   Close the database and do not save the changes.

Querying a Database

Querying is another way to locate records that contain specific information within a database. With a query, you can define exactly which records you seek. For example, you can find within the REALTYDB.WDB database only the records for houses that cost less than $150,000 or the ones with three or more bedrooms. You can combine criteria, too, and look for the houses that cost less than $150,000 *and* have three or more bedrooms. Some of the queries you can make:

- Search for records that contain an exact match to the text you are looking for, in the field where you expect to find it. Search for records that match in more than one field.

- Find only the records that contain text alphabetically before or after the text you enter in a query. You can also find records that contain a value greater than or less than the value you specify.

- Find the records that fall within a range of alphabetic or numeric values.

- Find all the records that do not match or do not fall within a range.

- Queries can be saved so you won't have to re-create them if you close and reopen a database.

Queries can also use calculations and dates.

To make a simple query, choose Tools, Create New Query or click the query icon (the one with the question mark). The *Query* dialog box appears. You use operators, text, and numbers to create your query. In the next activity you will find all the houses in the Hethwood subdivision that cost $150,000 or less.

Database

New Query

Please give this query a name: `Query1`

Create query sentences below, and then choose Apply Now to see all records that match the criteria.

Choose a field to compare:	**How to compare the field:**	**Value to compare the field to:**
A. `Subdivision` ⬍	B. `is equal to` ⬍	E. `Hethwood`

◉ And
○ Or

| F. `Price` ⬍ | G. `is less than` ⬍ | I. `150000` |

○ And
○ Or

| J. `_____` ⬍ | K. `_____` ⬍ | L. `_____` |

| Clear | Apply Now | Query View | Cancel | Help |

ACTIVITY 12.9

Making a Simple Query

1. Open the REALTYDB.WDB database from the student diskette.

2. Start a simple query and give it a name.

   click the List view icon

   click the Query icon to the right of the List view icon

   in the Please give this query a name *text box type* **Wilson**

3. Enter the initial criteria.

   in list box A. *click the arrow to display a list of the fields*

   choose the Subdivision field

   in list box B. *click the arrow to display a list of operators*

   choose is equal to

   in text box E. *type* **Hethwood** *(the name of the subdivision)*

   So far your query asks for a subdivision equal to Hethwood.

4. Add a second criterion to the query.

   click the And option button below box B.

   in box F. *choose the Price field*

   in box G. *choose less than or equal to*

   in box I. *type* **150000**

   Your complete query asks for a subdivision equal to Hethwood whose price is less than or equal to $150,000.

5. View the results.

   click the Apply Now button

   A list of homes appear that meet the criteria for the query. The list shows five records with Hethwood as the subdivision and $150,000 or less as a price. At the right end of the status bar Works shows 5/31, which signifies that five records of the 31 in the database meet the criteria you set for the query.

6. Close the database and **do save** the changes.

ACTIVITY 12.10
Using a Query

1. Open the REALTYDB.WDB database that you closed in the previous activity.

2. Use the previous query.

    choose View, Query

    click the Wilson query and press ⌷**ENTER**

    click the List view icon to view the homes

3. View the list in Form view.

    click the Form view icon

    The form for the first home appears.

    in the lower left corner of the window click the next record arrow

    The form for the next record meeting the criteria appears. The Status bar indicates record 9.

4. Delete the query.

    choose Tools, Delete Query

    choose the name Wilson and click Delete

    click OK

5. Close the database and **do save** the changes.

Making Queries with a Database Form

Using the New Query command and dialog box is a quick way to create a query but it has limitations. A more comprehensive approach is to enter your criteria directly into a query form, which resembles the database form. With a query form you type the criteria for the query directly into the data fields and then switch to List view to see the results.

Database

ACTIVITY 12.11

Using a Query Form

1. Open the ATLAS.WDB database.

2. Open a query form.

   choose Tools, Create New Query

   or

   click the Query icon

   click the Clear button to clear any existing entries

   click the Query view button to go to the query form

3. Enter the criteria.

   click the data entry portion of the Area field

   *type >**100000** and press* ⏎ENTER

   click the List view icon to see the results

   Eight records meet the criteria.

4. Name the query.

   choose Tools, Name Query

   click Query1 in the Queries box

   *type **Area** in the Name box*

   click the Rename button to rename Query1

   click OK

5. Close the database without saving the changes.

Rules for Making Queries

You select the records you want to view by typing conditions into the fields of a query form. Begin by clicking the Query icon. Clear any preexisting criteria with the Clear button and then click the Query view button for a query form.

⊖lf

- To select a record that contains text that exactly matches the query criteria, type the text into the field where the match is to be searched for. Queries do not look for embedded text like the Find command. If you want to find the Hethwood subdivision, you must type the full word Hethwood in the Subdivision field.

- To select records that match in more than one field, type each criteria in its appropriate field.

- To search for records that come before or after letters in the alphabetic or are greater or less than a number, use the conditional operators with the letters or numbers. When text is used with a conditional operator, it must be surrounded by double quotation marks.

Condition	Means	Example	Finds
=	equal to	="10"	The exact value of 10 only. Same as typing10 in the field.
>	greater than	>"H"	Any text Ha or beyond.
<	less than	<0.4	Less than 0.4.
>>=	greater than or equal to	>="H"	Any text H or beyond.
<<=	less than or equal to	<=150000	Equal to or less than 150,000.
<>	not equal to	<>9	Any value but 9.

You may also use the #AND# operator to find values within a specified range.

#AND#	and	>1#AND#<2	Greater than 1 and less than 2.
		>"H"#AND#<"K"	Words that begin H through J.

You may use the #AND# and the #OR# operator to find records that meet unusual criteria. For example, to find houses in either the Hethwood or Royal Oak subdivisions, type the following into the Subdivision area of the query form. The =*Subdivision* is required.

    =Subdivision="Hethwood"#OR#="Royal Oak"

The subdivision may be either Hethwood **or** Royal Oak.

Database

You may use & as another way to search with multiple criteria. For example, type in the Heat field (as a matter of fact, the query will work if you type the conditions into any field):

=Heat="Gas"#AND#Subdivision="Windsor"

The heat must be Gas and the subdivision Windsor.

- After you have defined a query Works retains the condition on the Query form. Save the query by name using Tools, Name Query if you plan to use the query again.

- You can also use wild cards with a query.

ACTIVITY 12.12
Using Multiple Criteria in a Query

1. Open the REALTYDB.WDB database.

2. Go to the Query form.

   click the Query icon

   click the Clear button and the Query view button

3. Find the houses in the range $180,000 through $200,000.

   in the Price field type **>=180000#AND#<=200000** *and press* ⏎ENTER

   click the List view icon

   Works lists five houses, including three that are $180,000.

   in the Price field change the criteria to **>180000#AND#<200000** *and press* ⏎ENTER

   click the List view icon

   Works leaves out the three houses at $180,000.

4. Find the houses in Windsor that do not have oil heat. First method.

   click the Query icon

   delete the criteria in the Price field

   in the Subdivision field type **Windsor**

in the Heat field type **<>"Oil"** *and press* 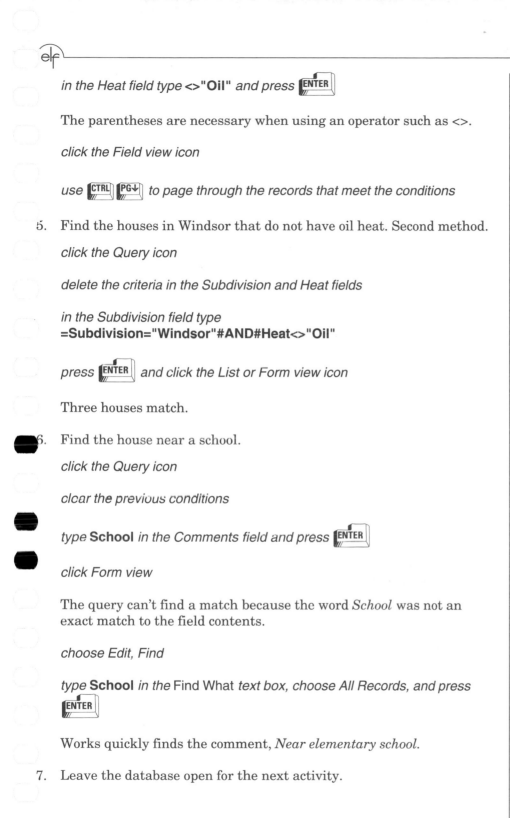ENTER

The parentheses are necessary when using an operator such as <>.

click the Field view icon

use CTRL PG↓ *to page through the records that meet the conditions*

5. Find the houses in Windsor that do not have oil heat. Second method.

   click the Query icon

   delete the criteria in the Subdivision and Heat fields

   in the Subdivision field type
   =Subdivision="Windsor"#AND#Heat<>"Oil"

   press ENTER *and click the List or Form view icon*

   Three houses match.

6. Find the house near a school.

   click the Query icon

   clear the previous conditions

   type **School** *in the Comments field and press* ENTER

   click Form view

   The query can't find a match because the word *School* was not an exact match to the field contents.

   choose Edit, Find

   type **School** *in the* Find What *text box, choose All Records, and press* ENTER

   Works quickly finds the comment, *Near elementary school.*

7. Leave the database open for the next activity.

Using Dates in a Query

Works can find dates if they are in a format that it recognizes and they are enclosed in single quotes (').

ACTIVITY 12.13
Working with Dates in a Query

1. Find the houses that have been on the market since the beginning of 1993.

   click the Query icon

   *in the Date on Market field type >***'1/1/93'*** and press* **ENTER**

   click the List view icon to view the results

   Twelve houses are listed. If you don't find any houses, make sure that you have cleared the conditions from the last query.

2. Leave the database open for the next activity.

Using Math with Queries

You can use the +, -, *, /, and ^ operators to perform mathematical operations with queries.

ACTIVITY 12.14
Using Math in a Query

1. Make sure REALTYDB.WDB is the active database.

2. Find the houses with a real estate tax exceeding $750 per year. The tax rate is $4.49 per $1,000 of assessed value.

   in the Price field type **=Price*4.49/1000>750**

   press  *and click the List view icon*

   Ten records are listed.

3. Close the REALTYDB.WDB database and do not save the changes.

Database Printing

If you just want to print a copy of the database, you can use the File, Print command. As with the other Works programs, you can add headers and footers and place page breaks. With the File, Page Setup and Margins command you can change the margins to position the database on the page. Use the Print Preview icon to look at the database the way it will be printed. Later you will learn how to print a database report where you can group fields and add totals at the end of the report.

◤ ACTIVITY 12.15

Printing a Database

1. Open the ATLASPOP.WDB database from the student diskette.

2. Use List view and sort the database in ascending order on the E/W field.

3. Get ready to print.

   click the Print Preview icon to view the way the database will be printed

   check to see if the entire database will fit on one page

   click Cancel

   choose File, Page Setup and click the Margins tab

   set the Top and Bottom margins to .9"

   again use Print Preview to see if margins need adjustment

4. Print.

   make sure the printer is on-line

   choose File, Print

5. Close the database and do not save the changes.

On Your Own

1. Open the ATLASPOP.WDB database.

2. Find the state with the tallest mountain east of the Mississippi River. Hint: Try sorting on the E/W and the Max El fields.

Database

3. Find the states with the largest area west of the Mississippi and east of the Mississippi.

4. Find the states with a population density greater than 500 people per square mile. Hint: Use a query with a mathematical expression.

5. Find the states with the maximum and minimum population densities. Hint: Create a new Pop Den field and sort on it.

6. Find the state whose capital is Trenton.

7. Find the states where the population growth has been less than 1 percent since 1980. Hint: Use the formula (Pop Now - Pop 1980)/Pop 1980<.01

8. Find the states where the population growth has been greater than 25 percent. Can you do it either with a query or by creating a new field and then sorting?

9. Find the difference in total population between 1980 and now.

Quick Check

1. How do you automatically fill in a field for every record?

2. What are the differences between using the Edit, Find command and using a query?

3. How do you calculate a running total?

4. Why might you sort a database on both primary and secondary keys?

5. How could you find the all the names beginning with the letters *Ro* in a database using Find? using a query?

6. How would you find all the names in a database that begin with an *R*, *S*, or *T*?

7. How would you find all the houses that cost between $100,000 and $150,000? What is the difference between the following queries?

=Price>100000#AND#<15000   =Price>=100000#AND#<=150000

8. What condition would you use to query a database with a date field for records between 1 July 1991 and 30 June 1992?

Writing a Database Report

13

Overview

Now that you can sort and search a database, you can put these tools to work in creating a database report. Database reports organize and summarize your data before printing. You can also arrange your report by groups based on fields with the same data, and add statistics. Works will lead you through the preparation of a simple report, then allow you to modify it to suit your needs.

Objectives

- Create a standard report
- Choose which fields to print and where they should appear on the page
- Add titles and comments
- Add statistics such as sums, counts, and averages to the report
- Group records by field entries
- Preview, save, and print the report

Creating a Standard Database Report

When you create a standard report, Works takes you through the process step by step. Choose Tools, Create New Report or click the Report icon to the right of the Query icon. The *New Report* dialog box looks like the one below.

- You can type in a report title in the *Report Title* text box. The title will appear at the top of the first page only.

- Choose the fields to be included in the report by selecting them one at a time from the *Fields in Report* list and then clicking the Add button. Click OK when you have added all the fields you want printed in the report.

Database

New Report

Report Title: DSR Employee Realty   OK

Field: Fields in Report: Cancel

Ser No   Address   Help
Address   Subdivision
Subdivision   Add >>   Bedrooms   To include
Bedrooms   Baths   fields in the
Baths   Remove   Lot Size   report, choose
Lot Size   Heat   fields in the
Heat   Add All >>   Age   Field box and
Age   choose the Add
Price   Remove All   button.
Date on Market

When you have finished with the first dialog box, Works displays a *Report
Statistics* box.

• Choose the fields, one by one, for which you would like summary
statistics. After you have chosen a field, click the *Statistics* check box
or boxes for the statistics you want shown at the bottom of the report.

• The statistics can be shown at the bottom of each column or grouped
in rows. Choose an option for your report.

Report Statistics

Select statistics to appear in report: OK

Fields in Report: Statistics   Cancel
Address   X Sum
Subdivision   X Average   Help
Bedrooms   Count
Baths   Minimum
Lot Size   Maximum   Position Statistics
Heat   Standard Deviation   ○ Under each column
Age   Variance   ● Together in rows
Price

When you click OK, an information box appears to tell you, *The report
definition has been created. To see what the report will look like when you
print, select Print Preview.* Click OK to see a window with the report
definition.

The report definition contains the information that will be printed in a
form that you can edit. Along the left side of the definition screen are a
list of instructions to tell Works what information is to be printed. It
includes a title, column headings, record, and summary rows. At the top
of the screen the report is divided into columns containing the fields you
chose to be included in the report.

	A	B	C	D	E	F	G	H
Title			DSR Employee Realty					
Title								
Headings	Address	Subdivision	Bedrooms	Baths	ot Siz	Heat	Age	Price
Headings								
Record	=Address	=Subdivision	=Bedroom	=Baths	=Lot S	=Heat	=Age	=Price
Summary								
Summary	AVERAGE Lot Size:		=AVG(Lot					
Summary	AVERAGE Age:		=AVG(Age					
Summary	TOTAL Price:		=SUM(Pric					
Summary	AVERAGE Price:		=AVG(Pric					

After you have created a report definition it should be saved. Works treats database reports in much the same way as the spreadsheet program does charts. The report definition is attached to the database. You can have as many as eight report definitions for each database.

You can also edit the definition by moving the location of the fields or the summary columns or formatting the results.

ACTIVITY 13.1

Creating a Report Definition

1. Open the REALTYDB.WDB database from the student diskette.

2. Create a report and give it a title.

    click the Report icon (to the right of the Query icon)

    or

    choose Tools, Create New Report

    type **DSR Employee Realty** *in the* Report Title *text box*

3. Add the fields you want in the report.

    select Address in the Field *list box and click Add*

    Works adds the field to the *Fields in Report* list and moves the selection to the next field.

    add the Subdivision, Bedrooms, Baths, Lot Size, Heat, Age, and Price fields to the list of Fields in Report

    click OK

4. Add statistics to the report.

    select the Lot Size field and mark the Average check box in the Statistics area

    select the Age field and mark the Average check box

    select the Price field and mark the Sum and the Average check boxes

    click OK twice to view the report definition

5. Give the report a name.

    choose Tools, Name Report

    Works proposes the name Report1.

    type **Basic** *in the* Name *text box*

    click Rename and click OK

    choose File, Save As and name the database **MYREPORT.WDB**

6. Preview the report.

    choose File, Print Preview or click the Preview icon

    Is the last column off the page?

    click Cancel

    choose File, Page Setup and click the Margins tab

    set the left and right margins to .8"

    adjust the column widths in the report so the column titles are not truncated

    click the Preview icon

    click the Print icon to print the report

7. Switch between List view and Report view.

    click the List view icon to switch to List view

    choose View, Report

    click Basic in the Report *list box*

click OK to return to Report view

8. Leave the database open for the next activity.

Editing and Formatting a Report

You can edit and format a report in much the same way that you edit and format a database. For example, to move the summary statistics to a new location, cut them from one column and paste them in another. To change the width of a column, drag the right edge of the column label. To format the summary values, select their placeholders (the functions shown in the place where values will print) and apply a format.

ACTIVITY 13.2

Editing Your Report

1. Make sure MYREPORT.WDB is the active database and switch to Report view.

   choose View, Report

   click Basic in the Report *list box*

   click OK to return to Report view

2. Move the Summary information.

   widen column C by dragging the border of the column label

   select the placeholders =AVG(Lot Size), =AVG(Age), =AVG(Price), and =SUM(Price) in column C

   note the row position for the top row of the selection

   choose Edit, Cut

   click the same row in column H

   choose Edit, Paste

   The summary information has been moved to column H.

3. Change the widths of the columns.

   alternate between the report definition and Print Preview to determine the proper widths for the columns

Database

in the report definition view, change the width of any column that needs adjustment by dragging the edge of the column label

4. Format the summaries.

   select the Lot Size placeholder and choose Format, Number, Fixed

   format with 1 decimal place

   format the Age placeholder the same way

   do the same for the Average Lot Size and the Average Age placeholders

   preview the report

5. Use the methods shown above to complete the report.

   move the title to column C

   Hint: use the cut and paste icons.

   move the Summary legends to column B

   format the Total Price placeholder as Currency with 0 decimal places

   click on the field containing AVERAGE *Lot Size:*

   edit the field to read **Average Lot Size:**

   do the same for the three Summary legends below it

   remove the underlines from the Headings and make them italic

6. Change column alignment.

   select columns Bedrooms, Baths, Lot Size, Heat, and Age

   choose Format, Alignment and give the columns a center alignment

7. Save the database.

8. Print and close the database.

Modifying a Report

You can change the way Works groups data in a report and have statistics printed for each group. In the report definition below you can see that two additional row types have been added, an Intr Subdivision type and a Summ Subdivision type. The row types that Works permits:

Row Type	Purpose
Title	The title of the report plus other text such as a subtitle. The title field prints only on the first page of the report. Insert a blank title row if you want a blank line between the title and the body of the report.
Heading	Text printed at the top of each page.
Record	Tells Works which fields are to be included in each report record.
Intr *fieldname*	Inserts headings before a group of records or a blank row. *Fieldname* is the name of the field Works uses to group the database. To group records in a report, the database must first be sorted on the field you wish to group by.
Summ *fieldname*	Produces a statistical summary for a group of records. The summary is printed after each group of records.
Summary	Produces a summary at the end of the database.

You may add rows of any type to modify the database to suit your needs. The definition in the figure below produces a report grouped on the Subdivision field of the REALTYDB.WDB database.

	A	B	C	D	E
Title	DSR Employee Realty				
Title			by Subdivision		
Title					
Intr Subdivisi	Address	Subdivision	Bedrooms	Baths	Price
Record	=Address	=Subdivision	=Bedrooms	=Baths	=Price
Summ Subdivisi		Average Value of Homes			=AVG(Price)
Summ Subdivisi		Total Value in Subdivision			=SUM(Price)
Summ Subdivisi					
Summary		Average Lot Size:			=AVG(Lot Size)
Summary		Average Age:			=AVG(Age)
Summary		Total Price:			=SUM(Price)
Summary		Average Price:			=AVG(Price)

ACTIVITY 13.3

Customizing Your Report

1. Open the REALRPRT.WDB database from the student diskette. The database already has the Basic report attached.

Database

2.   Open the report definition.

choose View, Report

double-click Basic

The report definition contains only a title, column headings, and the fields to be included in each record of the report. An extra Title and Headings row are included to place a blank line after the title and headings.

3.   Duplicate the report with a new name.

choose Tools, Duplicate Report

select Basic

type **MYREPORT** *in the* Name *box*

click the Duplicate button, then click OK

Use MYREPORT for the rest of the chapter.

4.   Add a subtitle.

click on the label in the second row named Title

choose Insert, Row/Column

select Title in the Type *list box and click OK*

A new Title row is inserted in the report definition.

click on the intersection of column C and the second Title row

type **by Subdivision**

press [ENTER] *to add the subtitle*

5.   Delete extra fields.

select columns E (Lot Size), F (Heat), and G (Age)

choose Insert, Delete Row/Column

6.   Add a field.

click in the third row (first Headings row) in the blank column E beside the word Baths *choose Insert, Field Name*

scroll through the Fields *list and select Price, then click OK to add the heading*

format the field names as bold and underlined and remove the italics

center align the field names

click two rows down in column E in the Record row beside the =Baths *entry*

choose Insert, Field Entry

select Price in the Fields *list and click OK to add the field*

format the Price column as Currency with 0 decimal places

7. Widen the fields.

    if necessary, drag the borders of the column labels until the full field names are visible

    click the Print Preview icon to view the way the report would be printed

8. Save the database and report.

    choose FIle, Save As and save the database and reports as REPORT2.WDB

9. Return to the report definition screen and leave the database open for the next activity.

    click the List or Form view buttons

Grouping Records by Fields

You can also arrange your database so records can be grouped on a common field entry.

ACTIVITY 13.4

Arranging the Report by Groups of Records

1. Sort the database on the Subdivision field. The report definition must be the active screen.

Database

*with the report definition MYREPORT on screen, choose Tools, Sort
Records*

in the 1st Field *list box choose* **Subdivision**

mark the Break G check box and leave the 1st Letter I check box clear

You would choose the 1st Letter check box if you wanted the grouping
to change for each first letter, all the A's together, a break and then
all the B's, etc.

click OK

A new row appears in the report definition, named Summ
Subdivision. This instruction will place summary statistics after each
group. Works has, by default, placed a count instruction for each text
column and a sum instruction for each numeric column.

2. View the report and change the summary statistics.

    click the Preview icon and note the arrangement of the report by groups

    The report is now arranged in groups according to entries in the
    Subdivision field. A summary statistic is placed at the bottom of each
    column based on the arrangement of the fields in the original report
    definition.

    click Cancel to return to the report definition screen

    *select the fields in the columns to the right of the Summ Subdivision label
    (row labeled Summ Subdivision, columns A through G), but **not** the
    Summ Subdivision label itself*

    choose Edit, Clear to clear the default definitions

    click column E in the Summ Subdivision row, under =Price

    choose Insert, Field Summary

    select the Price in the Fields *list and Avg as the* Statistics *option, then
    click OK*

    preview the report, then click Cancel

3. Add another summary row and statistic.

    click the top Summary label to select the entire row

    choose Insert, Row/Column

select Summ Subdivision and click OK

A blank Summ Subdivision row is inserted.

click the cell at the intersection of column E and the new row

choose Insert, Field Summary

select Price in the Fields _list and Sum as a Statistics option_

view your progress with Print Preview

click Cancel to return to the report definition

4. Leave the report definition open for the next activity.

ACTIVITY 13.5
Adding Headings and Labels

1. Add labels for the summaries.

   click the intersection of column B and the first Summ Subdivision row

   type **Average value of homes**

   click column B of the second Summ Subdivision row

   type **Total value in Subdivision**

   select the placeholders in column E for the labels and choose Format, Number

   choose a Currency format with 0 decimal places

2. Add headings for each group.

   At present, headings appear at the top of the page listing but not at the top of every group.

   click the second Headings label to select that row

   choose Insert, Delete Row/Column

   click the Record label to select that row

   choose Insert, Row/Column

   select Intr Subdivision and click OK

Database

3. Move the headings.

select fields A through E in the Headings row

choose Edit, Cut

click field A in the Intr Subdivision row

choose Edit, Paste to move the headings from the Headings row to the Intr Subdivision row

click the remaining Headings label to select the row

choose Insert, Delete Row/Column

review your work with Print Preview

4. Save your work and leave the report definition on screen for the next activity.

Activity 13.6
Completing the Report

1. Make sure that the report definition is the current window and change the top and bottom margins.

choose File, Page Setup and click the Margins tab

make the top and bottom margins .5"

2. Add a line between groups.

in the report definition window click the top Summary label to select the row

choose Insert, Row/Column

select Summ Subdivision and click OK

review the report with Print Preview

You've added a line between groups.

3. Delete the extra row at the bottom of the report.

click on the top Summary label

choose Insert, Delete Row/Column

4. Change a label.

   in the third Summary row replace Total Price *with* **Total Value of Real Estate:**

   review your work with Print Preview

5. Save and print the database report. Works prints the report or database that is currently on screen. The top half of your report should look like the one below.

6. Close the database.

DSR Employee Realty

by Subdivision

Address	Subdivision	Bedrooms	Baths	Price
12 Bartholomew Sq	Hethwood	5	4	$290,000
455 Daniels Rd	Hethwood	2	1	$47,500
45 Lyrwood Dr	Hethwood	3	2	$55,000
315 Fremont Ave	Hethwood	5	2	$160,000
19 Hill Rd	Hethwood	4	2	$110,000
131 Putnam Ave	Hethwood	3	2	$120,000
287 Carmel Terr	Hethwood	3	2	$194,000
194 Maplewood	Hethwood	3	1	$76,000
Average Value of Homes				$131,563
Total Value in Subdivision				$1,052,500

Address	Subdivision	Bedrooms	Baths	Price
903 Ray Rd	Long Lakes	2	1	$42,000
34 Home Pl	Long Lakes	7	5	$180,000
19 Auburn St	Long Lakes	4	2	$112,500
87 Newbury St	Long Lakes	6	2	$120,000
16 Rice St	Long Lakes	5	3	$180,000
1463 Woodlawn Ave	Long Lakes	3	2	$42,500
714 Orchard St	Long Lakes	5	3	$185,000
Average Value of Homes				$123,143
Total Value in Subdivision				$862,000

Database

Case Study

In this case study you will perform all the steps necessary to create, edit, sort, query, and write a database report.

Part 1.

1. Create a database with fields as shown below. The number shown in the field is the field length.

X4.17" Y4.08"	

DSR Employee Database

Last Name: 20   First Name: 15

Dept: 12   Emp No: 5

Salary: 10

Start Date: 10

2. Add the following records to the database.

Last Name	First Name	Dept	Emp No	Salary	Start Date
Price	Kenney	Contracts	967	$33,200	5/12/78
Jones	Sam	Contracts	150	$19,700	2/6/67
Zarco	Todd	Legal	674	$63,800	8/4/66
Ford	Charles	Admin	53	$29,500	4/10/84

3. Save the database with the name MYSTAFF.WDB. Close the database.

4. Open the database STAFF.WDB from the student diskette to save typing the remaining entries.

5. Sort the database by 1st key Last Name and 2nd key First Name in ascending order.

6. Insert a new field named Bonus in Form view. In List view, have the field calculate a 4 percent bonus for each employee.

7. Use a running total to find the total cost of the bonus.

8. Find the employee with the highest salary. The employee with the most service.

9. Use a query to list the employees who make between $25,000 and $50,000 per year.

10. Use a query to find the employees hired since 1/1/90.

11. Find the employees hired since 1/1/90 and who make more than $30,000.

12. Find the employee in each department who has worked the longest.

Part 2.

1. Create a database report grouped by department (Dept) showing the fields Last Name, First Name, Dept, Emp No, and Salary. Title the report *Salaries by Department*. At the bottom of the report have Works list the total, average, maximum, and minimum salary for the entire company with each statistic on a separate row. Have the report show the average and total salaries after each group with an appropriate legend. Place field headings before each group. Name the report *Salaries*.

2. Create a database report (Tools, Create New Report) that could be used as a phone book. Use the fields Last Name, First Name, Dept, and Ph Ext. Sort on a 1st Field of Last Name with the Break and 1st Letter options and a 2nd Field of First Name. Use the field names in a page heading. No statistics are needed. Title the report *DSR Phone Extensions*. Give the report a subtitle *DSR (802) 691-ext*. Name the report *Phone Book*.

3. Save the reports with the MYSTAFF.WDB database. Samples of the reports may be found on the student diskette with the file name STAFFRPT.WDB.

Quick Check

1. What two steps (dialog boxes) does Works use to create a basic report? How do you choose the fields that you want in your report? How do you choose the summary statistics you want to use?

2. How do you add a title to a report? modify the headings that Works add automatically? add an extra line under the report title?

Database

3. How do you tell Works to group the data in the report? add summaries of the group data? add group headings?

4. Describe how you would create a database for a phone book. Start with the factors to consider when you create the form. List the steps necessary to create a phone book using the database report definition.

Part IV
Making Works Work For You

In This Section

❑ *Move information from one Works application to another*

❑ *Use the Microsoft Draw applet to add graphics to your work*

❑ *Use the word processor and database programs to prepare form letters and mailing labels*

❑ *Use the communications program to connect to remote computers*

Integration

Programs Working Together

14

Overview

Although each Works 3.0 for Windows program has been treated as though it were isolated from the others, you've seen that they have many common elements. In this chapter you will see how the programs can work together.

Objectives

- Understand the purpose of the Windows 3.1 Clipboard
- Copy from Works to another Windows program
- Exchange data among the three Works programs
- Use the Works Draw program
- Add graphics to a document
- Understand mail merges
- Create a form letter and mailing labels

The Windows Clipboard

Whenever you cut or copy material from a Window's 3.1 program it's placed in a special area in memory called the **Clipboard**. The Clipboard holds the latest item that has been cut or copied from a Windows application. If you cut or copy something new, it overwrites the previous item. While material is stored in the Clipboard it is available for pasting. Because the Clipboard is a separate program, you can cut or copy information from one Windows application into the Clipboard and then paste it into another application. Word processor text, a range in a spreadsheet, a record in a database, and a graphic or a chart can all be moved or copied from one application to another through the Clipboard.

Integration

ACTIVITY 14.1

Copying Text Through the Clipboard

1. Open the document ACME.WPS from the student diskette.

2. Select text and copy it to the Clipboard.

    select the DSR address

> DSR Corporation
> 1236 Brighton Lane
> Bethesda, MD 22003

    choose Edit, Copy to place the address in the Clipboard

3. Leave Works temporarily and go to the Windows Program Manager.

    hold down **ALT** *and press* **TAB** *repeatedly until the Program Manager name and icon appear in a rectangle in the center of the screen*

    release the **ALT** *key to make the Program Manager active*

4. Start another Windows program.

    find the Notepad icon

    The Notepad is a simple word processor. You may have to maximize the Program Manager and the Accessories group to find the Notepad.

    double-click the Notepad icon to start the program

5. Copy the address into Notepad.

    choose Edit, Paste

    The address is copied to Notepad.

6. Close Notepad and return to Works.

    choose File, Exit and do not save the changes

hold down **ALT** *and press* **TAB** *repeatedly until the Works icon appears*

release the **ALT** *key to return to Works 3.0*

7. Close the document ACME.WPS and do not save any changes.

Copying Information Among Works Programs

You can also copy information among the three Works programs using Cut and Copy. The spreadsheet and database programs share a similar arrangement: columns and rows dividing the data into units. The corresponding arrangement in the word processor is a table with tab positions corresponding to the columns and paragraphs to the rows. The next activity will illustrate how you can copy data among the three programs. You will have several documents open at one time. Use the Window command or press [Ctrl] [F6] to quickly switch from one window to another.

ACTIVITY 14.2

Copying Among Programs

1. Open the document SCHTABS.WPS from the student diskette.

    choose View, All Characters to show the non-printing characters

    note the positions of the tab characters in the table

2. Select the data to copy.

    select the four paragraphs (lines) that form the body of the table

    choose Edit, Copy

3. Create a spreadsheet and paste the data.

    choose File, Create New File and click the Spreadsheet button

    click cell B3 in the new spreadsheet

    choose Edit, Paste

    The table is pasted into the spreadsheet, using the tabs from the document to separate the data into columns and the paragraph marks to separate the data into rows.

Integration

4. Create a database and paste the data.

   choose File, Create New File and click the Database button

   press the List view icon

   choose Edit, Paste Record

   The table from the document is pasted into the database. This time the tabs separate the data into fields and the paragraphs into records. Fields are given temporary names by Works. You should choose applicable field names (such as Origin, To, Destination, Fare, and Class) if you want to save the database.

5. Create a document and paste the data from the database.

   make List view active

   select the data in the four records of the database

   choose Edit, Copy

   choose File, Create New File and click the Word Processor button

   in the new document choose Edit, Paste

   Notice that the four records have been pasted as a table with tabs set left-aligned for text and right-aligned for numbers. Field names are not copied.

6. Close all the documents without saving any changes.

Linking Data from a Spreadsheet

When you paste data from a spreadsheet into a word processor document you may choose a special way of pasting. The data you paste can be linked to the original spreadsheet in such a way that when the spreadsheet is changed, the document is automatically changed as well. When you link data it's best to have both documents open.

ACTIVITY 14.3
Linking Data with Paste Special

1. Open the document REGSALES.WPS from the student diskette.

2. Open the spreadsheet REGSALES.WKS from the student diskette.

3. Select the table to copy to the document.

   select the range B5:C13 in the spreadsheet (including the blank cells)

   choose Edit, Copy

4. Paste Link the table into the document.

   press `CTRL` `F6` *to switch from the spreadsheet to the document*

   press `CTRL` `END` *to go to the end of the document*

   choose Edit, Paste Special

   in the Paste Special *dialog box select Microsoft Works 3.0 Sheet or Chart or Object and click the Paste Link option button*

   click OK

   Paste Special

   Source: Microsoft Works 3.0

   As:
   Microsoft Works 3.0 Sheet or Chart Object

   ○ Paste
   ● Paste Link

   [OK]
   [Cancel]
   [Help]

   ☐ Display As Icon

   Result
   Inserts a picture of the Clipboard contents into your document. Paste Link creates a link to the source file so that changes to the source file will be reflected in your document.

   After a few moments the table appears in the document. The complete set of gridlines will show in a printed document. If you don't want the gridlines, make the spreadsheet active and clear the View, Gridlines check mark. In the word processor, the table is treated as a single paragraph.

   click somewhere inside the table to select it

   click the Center alignment button to center the table

5. Change the data.

   change to the spreadsheet with `CTRL` `F6`

   in cell B13 type **Total**

Integration

in cell C13 click the Sum icon and press ENTER

format cell C13 as Currency with 0 decimal places

press CTRL F6 *to verify that the table has been automatically updated*

6. Leave the documents open for the next activity.

Adding a Spreadsheet Chart to a Document

You may want to enhance a document with a chart from the spreadsheet program. A chart can be copied directly to a word processor document.

ACTIVITY 14.4

Adding a Chart to a Document

1. Be sure that both REGSALES.WPS and REGSALES.WKS are open.

2. Prepare to copy the chart.

    make REGSALES.WPS the active document

    click to the right of the table added in the last activity

    press ENTER *twice to add two blank lines*

    press the Left align icon to make the paragraph left aligned

    type **Data from the table is shown in the chart below.**

    press ENTER *twice*

3. Insert an already created chart from REGSALES.WKS.

    be sure that REGSALES.WPS is still the active document

    choose Insert, Chart

    click REGSALES.WKS in the Spreadsheets *list box*

    The charts available with REGSALES.WKS are shown.

    click Revenue in the Charts *list box*

    click OK to insert the chart in the document

4. Change the chart size.

    select the chart by clicking somewhere inside it

    choose Format, Picture/Object

    in the Scaling area type **80** *in the* Width *box*

    type **60** *in the* Height *box and click OK*

    click the Center alignment icon

5. Print the document. Close both REGSALES files without saving the changes (or save them using different names).

Embedded Objects

Objects, such as drawings, that are created in other applications may be embedded in a Works word processor document if the application supports embedding. Works comes with such a program called Microsoft Draw. It was installed on your PC at the same time as Works.

When you embed an object in a document it remains linked to the application in which you created it. By double-clicking the object you return to the originating application. After making changes, you can return to Works and the object will be automatically updated.

ACTIVITY 14.5
Embedding an Object in a Document

1. Create a word processor document.

2. Add text and save the document.

    type **These are the two types of floppy diskettes in use today.** *at the top of the document*

    press [ENTER] *twice to add two blank lines*

    save the document on the student diskette with the name FLPYDISK.WPS

3. Start Draw from within Works.

    choose Insert, Drawing

    In a few moments the Microsoft Draw program starts.

Integration

4. Import clipart to the drawing

   in the Draw menu choose File, Import Picture

   change to the A: drive in the Directories *list box*

   double-click DISK35.WMF to import the drawing

   choose File, Import Picture

   double-click DISK525.WMF

5. Arrange the diskettes.

   click the drawing of the 5.25" diskette and drag it to the left

   click the drawing of the 3.5" diskette and drag it to the right so the diskettes are side by side

   choose File, Exit and Return to FLPYDISK.WPS

   answer Yes to Update FLPYDISK.WPS

   The Draw program disappears and the Works document appears with the drawing in place. As with a chart, Works treats an object as a paragraph.

6. Center the drawing.

   click within the drawing to select it

   click the Center alignment Icon

7. Leave the document open for the next activity.

ACTIVITY 14.6

Updating an Embedded Object

1. Add a border to the drawing.

   double-click the drawing

   In a few moments the Draw program appears with the drawing in place.

2. Draw a border around the diskettes.

   click the Rectangle tool (sixth tool from the top)

drag a border around the diskettes

The border is an opaque rectangle that overlays the diskettes.

choose Edit, Send to Back to place the border behind the diskettes

select the border

The border is selected when it shows small black handles at the corners. If the border is not selected, click it until the handles appear. If more than one object is selected, click outside the objects to remove the handles, then select the single object.

choose Draw, Line Style

choose a 2-point border

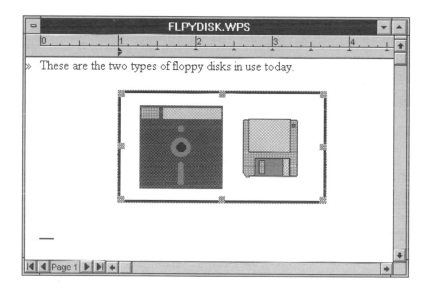

3. Update the drawing in the document.

in the Draw menu choose File, Update

choose File, Exit and Return to FLPYDISK.WPS

4. Save and print the document if you wish, then close the document.

Integration

On Your Own

1. Create a new document with the word processor. Title the document *The Four I States* and center the title. Press [Enter] twice and type the following: **Here are some statistics about the four states that begin with the letter I**. Save the document with the name ISTATES.WPS.

2. Open the ATLAS.WDB database from the student diskette. Use a query to find the states that start with the letter I. Hint: Type **>"I"#AND#<"J"** in the State field.

3. Select the four records and copy them to the word processor document ISTATES.

4. In the document, use the ruler to move the tabs so the table will fit on the page attractively. (Don't forget to select the entire table before setting tabs.) Delete the serial numbers at the beginning of each record. Add headings for the records.

5. In a similar manner, create a new spreadsheet and copy the records to it. Delete columns A, C, D, and E (No, Abv, Capital, and E/W).

6. Insert a new row 1 at the top of the spreadsheet. In row 1, label the columns State, Area, Population, Highest El.

7. Select the range A1:B5. Create a line chart from the selected data. Copy the chart to the document ISTATES.

8. Edit your document for the best appearance, then save and print.

9. Close all files.

Form Letters and Print Merging

With a print merge you can merge a database of names and addresses with a form letter to produce bulk mailings and mailing labels. There are two essential elements necessary for a **document merge**. The first is the form letter. This document contains the pattern that is common to each merged letter. The pattern document is frequently called the primary document and is created with the Works word processor. The second element is a listing of all the data that will change from one copy of the pattern document to the next. This information is contained in a Works database.

The Database Document

The database contains a listing of the data, which changes from one copy of the form letter to the next. Each record in the database contains the information to produce a single form letter. Each field to be inserted into the pattern document is represented by a placeholder. The placeholder consists of the field name surrounded by special characters that tell Works not to use the name literally, but to substitute a value from the database instead. Two typical database records are shown below:

	Last Name	First Name	Address	City	St	Zip	Telephone
1	Williams	Albert	234 Front St.	Frontier	OR	23456	(812) 341-2234
2	Robinson	Anne	169 Ferndale Dr., Apt 4	Westview	IN	41322	(815) 664-9071

When the data is used in a merge, the information from a single field is placed in the merged document at a location determined by the position of that field's placeholder in the pattern document. Each part of the record that you need to appear separately in the form letter should be made a different field.

The Form Letter

The primary document consists of text that is to appear in every form letter or label, plus placeholders for data from fields in the database. Here is an example that would produce an address, city, state, and zip code:

«ADDRESS»
«CITY», «ST» «ZIP»

Notice that the comma and spaces are added just as they would appear had you typed the address. The « and » symbols are added by Works to designate placeholders. An example of a simple form letter to use with the database is shown on the next page.

Integration

MEMO

FROM: Angela Williams

TO: «FIRST NAME» «LAST NAME»

DATE: *current date*

SUBJECT: Company Picnic

Dear «FIRST NAME»,

The DSR Corporation will hold its company picnic this year at the old Tollson farm. Because the 4th of July falls on a Saturday this year, we will hold the picnic on Friday the 3rd of July from 2 p.m. until the food runs out.

The picnic is for everyone, and all employees of the DSR Corporation are urged to attend. I hope to see the «LAST NAME» family on the 3rd.

Angela Williams

Coordinator

In the pattern document, you do not have to use every field in the database, and, if you wish, you can use a field more than once.

ACTIVITY 14.7

Creating the Database

1. Create a database.

2. Add two fields to the database.

    create a **Last Name** *field with a width of 20*

    create a **First Name** *field with a width of 15*

3. Add three names to the database in the appropriate fields.

Last Name	First Name
Robinson	Anne
Smithfield	Virginia
Ronson	Albert

4. Save the database.

choose File, Save As and save the database with the name MYNAMES.WDB

5. Leave the file open and go on to the next activity.

In the next activity you will create the primary document based on the earlier picnic memo. Works will let you insert fields from any open database using the Insert, Database Field command.

ACTIVITY 14.8
Creating the Primary Document

1. Create a word processor document.

2. Begin the memo.

type the text below using Times New Roman, 18 point, bold for the centered title and 12 point for the remaining text

MEMO¶

FROM: →   **Angela Williams**¶

¶

TO:

3. Add tabs.

with the insertion point to the right of TO: *press* [TAB] *2 times*

4. Add the fields.

choose Insert, Database Field

click the Database button at the bottom of the dialog box

double-click MYNAMES.WDB in the Databases *list box*

The available fields in the database appear.

click First Name in the Fields *list box*

click the Insert button, then click Close

press [Spacebar] to add a space between words

Integration

choose Insert, Database Field

click Last Name in the Fields *list box*

click the Insert button and then click Close

press **ENTER** *2 times to complete the paragraph and add a blank line*

5. Complete the next section of the form letter.

type **DATE:** *and press* **TAB** *2 times*

choose Insert, Special Character

select the Print Long Date option and click OK

press **ENTER** *2 times*

The current date according to the clock in your computer will be substituted when you print.

6. Type the remainder of the document. Don't forget to add the two additional placeholders (database fields).

7. Complete and save the document.

use Print Preview to view the memo and vertically center the body of the document to suit your taste

save the form letter with the name MYFORM.WPS

8. Leave both the form letter and the database open for printing.

Merge Printing

It is usually a good idea to preview your merge before you print. This is particularly true if you have a large number of records in the database. To merge your form letter with the database, have the form letter as the active document. Choose File, Print Form Letters and choose the database you want to use.

ACTIVITY 14.9

Merge the Form Letter and the Database

1. Be sure both MYNAMES.WDB and MYFORM.WPS are open.

   choose Window from the menu and confirm that both names appear in the file list

   make MYFORM.WPS the active document

2. Preview the merge.

   choose File, Print

   in the Print *dialog box mark the Print Merge check box*

   click the Preview button

   The *Choose Database* dialog box appears.

   select MYNAMES.WDB as the database you want to merge with the form letter

   click OK

3. Review the letters.

   use the Zoom button and the Next button to view the other two letters

   click Cancel to return to the pattern document

   Proof the letters for mistakes and make corrections.

4. Save and print the form letters.

   choose File, Print

   click Print

   in the Print *dialog box mark the Print Merge check box*

   select the All option and click OK

   choose MYNAMES.WDB and click OK

5. Save and close all files.

Integration

Mailing Labels

Mailing labels use a special kind of pattern letter together with a database. In the pattern letter you create a single mailing label using placeholders inserted from the database together with any necessary punctuation. To create the mailing label document choose Tools, Envelopes and Labels and click the Mailing Labels tab. Insert fields into the label, choose a label size, and print the labels.

In general there are two kinds of mailing labels, those that come on 8.5" by 11" sheets for the laser printer and those with holes along the edges for dot matrix printers.

Many laser printers can't print in a 0.25" margin around a sheet. After you've created the label form, you can adjust the margins using the *Page Size & Label Margins* dialog box. To check if the margins need adjustment, print a page of labels on a plain sheet of paper and match the labels on the sheet with the ones on a label page. Hold them up to the light to make sure the labels fall within the boundaries.

Avery Dennison is a company that produces labels for most printers. Each Avery label size has a number assigned. Works uses the Avery numbers to help you choose the right label for your needs.

Some common label sizes:

$1/2$" x $1^3/4$"   1" x $2^5/8$"   1" x 4" $1^1/3$" x 4"

CAUTION: If you intend to use a laser printer to produce labels, it is essential to choose labels designed for use in laser printers. Failure to do so can result in serious damage to the printer from the label adhesive. Laser labels also have a border to allow for the non-printing area in a laser printer.

In the next activity you will create mailing labels for a laser printer. The labels will be three across. This is the format used by Avery 5160 (or an equivalent brand) laser printer labels. If you use a different label, choose the appropriate number from the *Mailing Labels* dialog box.

Envelopes and Labels

_E_nvelopes	**_M_ailing Labels**

Enter the address, and choose a label style.

Label:

```
«Name»
«Address»
«City», «St»  «Zip»
```

_C_reate Label

Cancel

_H_elp

Choose the Fields button to include database fields on your envelope or label.

Label _s_tyle:

Avery 5160 [1" x 2 5/8"]

C_u_stom Label...

Fields>>

Current database:

LABLDATA.WDB

Data_b_ase...

_F_ields:

```
Name
Address
City
St
Zip
```

_I_nsert

To insert a field, select the field, then choose Insert.

ACTIVITY 14.10

Creating Mailing Labels

1. Open the database to use with the labels.

   open the database LABLDATA.WDB from the student diskette

2. Create the mailing label document.

   choose File, Create New File

   click the Word Processor button

   save the new label document with the name MYLABELS

3. Start creating the label.

   with MYLABELS as the active document choose Tools, Envelopes and Labels

Integration

click the Mailing Labels tab

click the Fields button

The dialog box expands for database selection and field entry.

click the Database button and select the LABLDATA.WDB database

click OK and return to the Mailing Labels *dialog box*

4. Add the fields.

   click the Name field in the Fields *list box, then click Insert*

   The Name field appears in the label.

   press E *to go to the next line*

   click the Address field in the Fields *box, then click Insert*

   press E *to go to the next line*

   in like manner insert the City field followed by a comma and a space

   insert the St field, two spaces, and the Zip field

5. Choose a label size and finish the label document.

   in the Label style *list box choose Avery 5160 (1" x 2⅝")*

   click the Create Label button

   The label appears in the document followed by a dotted line.

6. Print the labels on plain paper.

   choose File, Print

   in the Print *dialog box mark the Mailing Labels option button*

   mark the Print Merge check box

   click OK

   select the LABLDATA.WDB database in the Choose Database *dialog box*

   click OK a final time to print the labels

7. Compare the plain paper labels with an Avery 5160 laser printer label sheet. If the margins are not quite right choose File, Page Setup and click the Margins tab to adjust the margins to fit the sheet of labels, then try again.

8. Close all documents without saving any changes.

On Your Own

In this On Your Own you will take an existing document and turn it into a form letter. You will use a table in the document to create a database for use with the form letter.

1. Open the document OYOMLET.WPS from the student diskette.

2. At the bottom of the page is a table of names and addresses. Create a database. Cut the table from OYOMLET.WPS and paste it in the new database.

3. Give the fields appropriate names.

4. Return to OYOMLET.WPS and insert placeholders using the names from the database in the places where italicized words now appear in the form letter.

5. Print the letters.

6. Create a mailing label document and print labels.

7. Save the resulting documents with new names if you choose. Close OYOMLET.WPS without saving any changes.

Quick Check

1. What is the Windows 3.1 Clipboard? Of what use is it?

2. What steps allow you to copy database information into the word processor? In the word processor, how are the fields and records portrayed?

Integration

3. What two Works programs can be linked? How is linking different from cutting and pasting? How do you update a link?

4. What is an embedded object and how do you add it to a word processor document?

5. What two essential elements are there to a print merge? What two Works programs do you use?

6. What is a placeholder in a pattern document? How does it relate to a data document?

7. Briefly describe the steps in creating mailing labels.

Communications

15

Overview

Works 3.0 enables you to connect your computer to another computer to exchange information. You can send or receive files, conduct business such as electronic shopping, or view information on a service such as Compuserve or America Online.

NOTE: To send and receive information through a phone line, a modem (either internal or external) must be connected to your computer.

Objectives

- Create a communications file
- Adjust your communications settings
- Send a file
- Capture text
- Receive a file
- Record and play back a script

Communicating with a Remote Computer

NOTE: Your instructor will provide the telephone number and login information for the remote computer/service.

In the following activities, you will establish communications, adjust your settings, send a file to the remote computer, capture text from the remote computer, receive a file, and record a script that will make the communications process easier.

Integration

Creating a Communications File

The first step in communicating with another computer is to create a communications file.

From the *Startup* dialog box, click the Communications button. Works opens a new communications document and displays the *Easy Connect* dialog box.

```
┌─────────────────────────────────────────────────────────┐
│ ⊟                    Easy Connect                        │
├─────────────────────────────────────────────────────────┤
│ To connect to another computer,  type in the phone number  ┌────────┐ │
│ (with the prefix if necessary), then choose OK.  Name the  │   OK   │ │
│ service to identify it for future use.   When you save this file, it  └────────┘ │
│ will appear in the list below.                            ┌────────┐ │
│                                                           │ Cancel │ │
│ Phone number:        │555-5555              │             └────────┘ │
│                                                           ┌────────┐ │
│ Name of service:     │DSR Home Office       │             │  Help  │ │
│                                                           └────────┘ │
│ ─────────────────── OR ───────────────────               │
│ Select one of the services below and choose OK.          │
│ Services:                                                │
│ ┌──────────────────────────────────────────┐▲           │
│ │                                          │            │
│ │                                          │            │
│ │                                          │▼           │
│ └──────────────────────────────────────────┘            │
└─────────────────────────────────────────────────────────┘
```

NOTE: If this is the first time you have used the communications tool, Works displays the *Modem Setup* dialog box. Click the Test button to verify that your modem is properly connected and responding correctly to commands. Change settings, if necessary, and retest. When finished, click OK. Works will then display the *Easy Connect* dialog box.

In the *Phone Number* text box, type the number you want to dial. In the *Name of Service* text box, type the name of the person, organization, or service you want to call. After you save the document, this name will appear in the Phone Menu and in the *Easy Connect* dialog box in the *Services* list. Click the OK button and Works dials the number. Works displays the *Dial Status* dialog box to show the progress of the connection being made.

```
┌─────────────────────────────────────────────────────────┐
│ ⊟                    Dial Status                         │
├─────────────────────────────────────────────────────────┤
│ Connecting to:  555-5555                   ┌──────────┐  │
│ ┌Status──────────────────────────────────┐ │  Cancel  │  │
│ │                                        │ └──────────┘  │
│ │ Dialing phone number: 555-5555    45   │ ┌──────────┐  │
│ │                                        │ │   Help   │  │
│ └────────────────────────────────────────┘ └──────────┘  │
└─────────────────────────────────────────────────────────┘
```

When you are connected to the other computer, type your user identification and password, if required.

To disconnect from the remote computer, click the Dial/disconnect button in the Toolbar.

ACTIVITY 15.1

Start the Communications Program

1. Start Works 3.0 by clicking the Microsoft Works icon in the Program Manager.

2. Start the communications program.

    if the Startup *dialog box appears, click the Communications button*

    or

    if the Startup *dialog box does not appear, choose File, Create New File*

    click the Communications button in the dialog box

    The communications program starts and presents a new document.

ACTIVITY 15.2

Create a Communications File

1. Type the information about the service you want to access into the *Easy Connect* dialog box.

    in the Phone Number *text box, type the remote computer/service's phone number*

    press

    in the Name of Service *text box, type a description for the remote computer/service*

    click OK

    Works dials the number you entered.

Integration

2.   Enter the login information as needed.

type your user identification

press

type your password, if necessary

press

You are now connected to the remote computer/service.

3.   Disconnect from the remote computer/service.

follow logoff instructions from the remote computer/service

click the Dial/disconnect button

click OK in the OK to disconnect? *dialog box*

4.   Save the communications document.

choose File, Save As

choose the A: drive in the Save As *dialog box*

type **MYCOMM1** *in the* File Name *text box and click OK*

5.   Leave the document open for the next activity.

Changing Settings

Computers exchanging information must be set up to follow the same rules. These rules include the speed at which data is transferred, the type of protocol (method of transfer), and the type of terminal with which you are communicating. Choose Settings from the menu and then pick the setting you need.

Choose Settings, Phone if you want to change the information about the phone number or name of the service you are calling. You can also set the number of times you want your modem to redial the number and how long to wait between tries. Or you can set your modem to automatically answer an incoming call from another computer.

Choose Settings, Communication if you want to change the information about which serial port your modem is connected to, the speed at which information is exchanged, and other settings that specify the way data should flow between computers. By default, Works uses the settings that are used by most information services. These settings may need to be changed if you are communicating with other computers such as mainframes.

Choose Settings, Terminal if you want to change the information about what kind of terminal you are connecting to and how you want Works to display characters on the screen.

Choose Settings, Transfer to select the transfer protocol for sending or receiving a file. This must match the protocol used by the other computer. You can also set the drive and directory where you want files to be stored when they are transferred to your computer.

Settings			
Phone	Communication	Terminal	**Transfer**

When you are transferring files between computers, you need to define the language the computers will speak. If you do not know the language, the communication service you are connected to should be able to tell you.

OK

Cancel

Help

Transfer protocol:

Kermit
XMODEM/CRC
YMODEM
ZMODEM

Text Transfers

Line Delay: 0

Choose Directory for a list of places to store this file.

Receive Directory:

C:\MSWORKS

Directory

ACTIVITY 15.3

Changing the Transfer Settings

1. Be sure MYCOMM1.WCM is the active document.

2. Prepare to change the transfer settings.

   choose Settings, Transfer

3. Change the transfer protocol.

   select ZMODEM from the Transfer Protocol *list box*

4. Set the directory in which you want files to be stored.

   click the Directory button

Integration

5. Select a drive.

    click inside the Drives *list box*

    A list of drives appears. You should have an A: and a C: drive, and you may have other drives as well.

    select the A: drive in the list box

    click OK

    The A: drive becomes the active drive. This step may take a few seconds. Under the word *Directories* at the top of the dialog box you will see **a:\.** This shows the drive and directory in which the file will be saved. The "\" stands for the root directory. If you get an error message regarding the drive, you may not have the diskette in place or the drive lever closed.

6. Save the settings.

    click OK to save the settings

7. Save the changes to the communications file.

    click the Save button in the Toolbar

Sending Files

You can send a file such as a word processor document or a spreadsheet to another computer using the communications program. This is useful when you want to share a Works document or other file.

There are two types of files you can send. The first is a **text file** (also called an ASCII file). A text file cannot contain any formatting such as bold characters, indents, or centered text. The other type of file is a **binary file** such as Works documents. These can contain all the formatting that controls how a word processing document or a spreadsheet is printed.

To send a file, connect to the remote computer/service and indicate that you want to send (upload) a file. Choose Tools, Send File.

ACTIVITY 15.4

Send a File

1. Be sure MYCOMM1.WCM is the active document.

2. Connect to the remote computer/service.

    choose Phone, Dial

    Works dials the number.

3. Enter the login information.

    type your user identification

    press

    type your password, if necessary

    press

    You are now connected to the remote computer/service.

4. Follow any instructions on the screen from the remote computer/
    service about sending (or uploading) a file.

5. Begin sending your file.

    choose Tools, Send File

    or

    click the Send Binary File button in the Toolbar

6. Select the file you want to send from the *Send File* dialog box.

    select Drive A:

    select APREYNO.WPS (or another file designated by your instructor)

    click OK

    Wait for the file transfer to be completed.

Integration

7. Disconnect from the remote computer/service.

follow logoff instructions from the remote computer/service

click the Dial/disconnect button

click OK in the OK to disconnect? *dialog box*

Receiving Text and Files

Now that you've sent information to the remote computer, it would be nice to get something back.

There are two ways you can save information from a remote computer/service. One is to capture text that appears on your screen and save it in a file. This is useful if you are viewing more information than will fit on one screen or for saving an E-mail message. Another way is to receive a file (download) from the remote computer/service.

Capturing Text

To capture incoming text to a file, connect to the remote computer/service. Choose Tools, Capture Text. Type the filename where you want the captured text stored in the *File Name* text box.

ACTIVITY 15.5
Capture Text

1. Be sure MYCOMM1.WCM is the active document.

2. Connect to the remote computer/service.

   choose Phone, Dial

   Works dials the number.

3. Begin to capture the text of your login procedure.

   choose Tools, Capture Text

   or

   click the Capture Text button on the Toolbar

4.   Type the name of the file in which you want to save the captured text.

choose Drive A:

type **MYLOGIN.TXT** *in the* File Name *text box*

5.   Enter the login information as needed.

type your user identification

press  **ENTER**

type your password, if necessary

press **ENTER**

6.   Stop capturing the text.

choose Tools, End Capture Text

or

● *click the Capture Text button on the Toolbar*

7.   Disconnect from the remote computer/service.

follow logoff instructions from the remote computer/service

● *click the Dial/disconnect button*

● *click OK in the* OK to disconnect? *dialog box*

Receiving a File

You can receive and save a file from a remote computer/service. This can either be a text file or a binary file. To receive a file, after you have connected to the remote computer/service, choose Tools, Receive File.

ACTIVITY 15.6

Receiving a File

1.   Be sure MYCOMM1.WCM is the active document.

2.   Connect to the remote computer/service.

choose Phone, Dial

Works dials the number.

Integration

3. Enter the login information as needed.

4. Follow the instructions on the screen from the remote computer/
    service for receiving (downloading) a file.

    type **APREYNO.WPS** *(or file name designated by instructor) when*
    prompted to enter a filename

5. Begin to receive the file.

    choose Tools, Receive File

    or

    click the Receive Binary File button on the Toolbar

    Wait for the file transfer to be completed.

6. Disconnect from the remote computer/service.

    follow logoff instructions from the remote computer/service

    click the Dial/disconnect button

    click OK in the OK to disconnect? *dialog box*

    To view the received file, choose File, Open Existing File and select
    APREYNO.WPS.

Scripts

Communication scripts allow you to record actions that are repetitive,
such as a sign-on sequence or accessing a certain type of information on a
remote computer/service. You can play the script back whenever you need
to perform the same task again. You can only record one sign-on script in
a communications document. You can record as many scripts as you like
for performing other tasks.

Record Script

Type of script:
  ● Sign-on   ○ Other

Script Name: [   ]

OK
Cancel
Help

ACTIVITY 15.7

Recording a Script of a Sign-on Sequence

1. Be sure MYCOMM1.WCM is the active document.

2. Begin to record the script of your sign-on sequence.

   choose Tools, Record Script

   click the Sign-on radio button and click OK

3. Connect to the remote computer/service.

   choose Phone, Dial

   Works dials the number.

4. Enter the login information.

   type your user identification

   press ENTER

   type your password, if necessary

   press ENTER

5. End the script.

   choose Tools, End Recording

6. Disconnect from the remote computer/service.

   follow logoff instructions from the remote computer/service

   click the Dial/disconnect button

   click OK in the OK to disconnect? dialog box

7. Save the changes to the communications file.

   click the Save button in the Toolbar

Integration

ACTIVITY 15.8

Playing Back a Script of a Sign-on Sequence

1. Be sure MYCOMM1.WCM is the active document.

2. Begin to play back the script of your sign-on sequence.

   choose Tools, Sign-on

   The script will dial the remote computer/service and perform the login procedure.

3. Disconnect from the remote computer/service.

   follow logoff instructions from the remote computer/service

   click the Dial/disconnect button

   click OK in the OK to disconnect? *dialog box*

Quick Check

1. Now that you have used the communications tool, what dialog box allows you to enter the phone number and name of the sevice you want to contact?

2. What are the two types of files you can send to a remote computer/ service?

3. What type of script would you use to record your procedure for connecting to another computer? How many of these can you have in a communications file?

4. What other type of script can you use? How many can you have in a communications file?

5. What setting determines the method by which files are transferred?

6. What command saves the text that appears on the screen when you are connected to a remote computer/service?

Integration

Index